LEADING
FROM THE
MIDDLE

SCOTT MAUTZ

LEADING
FROM THE
MIDDLE

A PLAYBOOK FOR MANAGERS TO INFLUENCE
UP, DOWN, AND ACROSS THE ORGANIZATION

WILEY

Published by John Wiley & Sons, Inc., Hoboken, New Jersey.
Published simultaneously in Canada.

For general information on our other products and services or for technical support, please contact our Customer Care Department within the United States at (800) 762-2974, outside the United States at (317) 572-3993 or fax (317) 572-4002.

Wiley also publishes its books in a variety of electronic formats. Some content that appears in print may not be available in electronic formats. For more information about Wiley products, visit our website at www.wiley.com.

Library of Congress Cataloging-in-Publication Data:

ISBN 9781394331680 (Paperback)
ISBN 9781119717881 (ePDF)
ISBN 9781119717942 (ePub)

Cover Design: Wiley
Cover Image: © CurvaBezier/Getty Images
Author Photo: Rick Norton

SKY10097562_013025

To Deb and Emma:
For inspiring me through the ups, downs, and acrosses in my life.

CONTENTS

INTRODUCTION

I t was a yellow fish with bright blue stripes, unlike any other in the aquarium, that drew my attention.

Regally, intentionally, it circled the center of the glass encasement at a measured pace, surrounded by myriad other fish darting wildly about. My co-worker, sitting next to me at a noisy work-dinner party, asked what I was staring at. I brushed the question off and reentered the fray of conversation, albeit half-heartedly. At a time when I felt frazzled in my middle management role, I kept stealing glances at the Pisces protagonist, my mind lost in association.

I was that fish.

Maneuvering in the middle of an oversized fishbowl, all eyes privy to my every movement. Surrounded, yet lonely. Pressure from all sides; the weight of water. Watching other fish with their own agenda zip by while I labored to remain steady and purposeful in the middle of it all.

Such is the plight of the middle manager, of those who lead from the middle.

Which would be anyone who has a boss or is a boss, at any level, anyone who must influence in all directions to do their job well.

Me. You.

My existential moment happened in the middle of my three-decade corporate career. Even as I moved closer to the "top" at Procter & Gamble to run multibillion-dollar businesses, I was still always in the middle at some level, with people to influence above, and always plenty of those to influence down and across. It was exhausting at times, exhilarating at others. I found myself wishing someone would study the unique challenges of middle managers and offer help. Then I decided, "Why not me?"

And so began a journey that carried on for 15 more years in corporate; intensely studying those who lead from the middle and their challenges, watching how they operate effectively (or not), learning the success secrets of influencing up, down, and across, all as I rose at P&G, knowing that understanding the middle was how I was able to rise at all to begin with.

It became a mission, a mission for the middle, one that has carried over into my post-corporate life. I leverage each class I teach as faculty at Indiana University's Kelley School of Business for Executive Education to study the middle manager. I conduct studies, interviews, surveys, and focus groups with these heroes. I wrote hundreds of articles about middle-management struggles for my top *Inc.com* column, garnering well over a million clicks a month, which speaks to the unmet need in this arena. I wrote the multi-award-winning books *Make It Matter* and *Find the Fire* that speak to leadership and self-leadership, all while harboring a burning desire to write the book that addresses head-on the challenges that middle managers face.

Which brings us to here.

I've been where you are. I know how challenging it is to have to influence in every direction, saddled with an undoable workload, often under-resourced, under-appreciated, and over-stressed. Surrounded, but alone.

It's time the specific challenges of middle managers are recognized and specific help is provided. And while I know the experience, research, data, and volumes of work poured into this book will serve you well, there's another reason it will become your playbook for leading from the middle.

Because it comes from the middle. My heart.

1 The Unique Challenges of Those Who Lead from the Middle

A t one point, any mid-level manager who worked for the Lego company had the set of directives in Figure 1.1 hanging on their office or cubicle wall.[1]

The middle is messy, full of contradictions and opposing agendas, and couldn't be more critical for a company's success.

And it's you. Those who lead from the messy middle work in spots higher or lower in the organization, from Vice Presidents, General Managers, and Directors to Sales, Marketing, and Design Managers, and many more. They have a boss and are a boss, at any level. It's anyone who has to lead up, down, and across an organization.

Don't be fooled by the old Dilbert cartoons or *Office* reruns. Those who lead from the middle, let's use the often-derogatory term "middle management" for a moment, aren't the go-nowhere, has-been, mediocre bureaucrats that block progress as popularized in pop culture. They're the ones that love what they do (mostly) and whose passion and talents make the company hum. They account for

Lead...and keep yourself in the background.
Build a close relationship with staff...and keep a suitable distance.
Trust your staff...and keep an eye on them.
Be tolerant...and know how you want things to function.
Keep your department's goals in mind...and be loyal to the whole firm.
Do a good job of planning your time...and be flexible with your schedule.
Freely express your view...and be diplomatic.
Be a visionary...and keep your feet on the ground.
Try to win consensus...and be decisive.
Be dynamic...and be reflective.
Be sure of yourself...and be humble.

Figure 1.1 Lego Directives

Source: Adapted from P. Evans, "Management 21C," Chapter 5, Financial Times, Prentice Hall (2000), in "Emerging Leadership: A Handbook for Middle Manager Development" (IDeA).

22.3 percent of the variation in revenue in an organization, more than three times that attributed to those specifically in innovation roles, according to Wharton research.[2] A five-year study from Stanford and Utah universities found that replacing a poor middle manager with a good one boosted productivity 12 percent, more than adding an incremental worker to a team.[3]

Those leading from the middle are the key to employee engagement. They interact with the largest part of the organization and have the most direct impact on attracting and retaining talent. In fact, research shows that employees who have strong middle leaders are 20 percent less likely to quit their job if offered more money from another company.[4] The Boston Consulting Group defined mid-level managers as "vital to success," according to their massive survey of executives spanning 100 countries that found nearly two-thirds of respondents said middle managers were more critical than top managers.[5]

Whether you lead from the upper middle, mid-middle, or way lower middle, if you have a boss and are a boss, if you lead up, down, and across an organization, take pride in your career-making position. And know the best realize that being in a position in the middle doesn't mean being stuck in the middle.

It means a chance to lead.

Marty Lyons, legendary former player and longtime radio announcer for the New York Jets football team, would know. Lyons played for the Jets for twelve seasons and led from the messy middle. Literally.

Lyons was a middle lineman sandwiched in between outside linemen Mark Gastineau and Joe Klecko, who along with Abdul Salaam, made up the famous "New York Sack Exchange," a group that led the NFL in sacks three times between 1981 and 1984.[6] Lyons told me on leading from the middle, "You have to know and embrace where you are and realize that being in the middle is a blessing. It means you have the opportunity to lead in all directions."

Lyons knew that his role as the middle lineman was to lock up the guys on the opposing front line so that the speedy outside linemen Gastineau and Klecko could get the edge in rushing the quarterback. He wanted to lead from the messy middle so the entire team could lead on the scoreboard. Later on, as Klecko, the locker room leader, got older, Lyons began stepping up to passionately yell and scream and psych his fellow players up before a game. Being in the middle always means the chance to lead, it just requires a keen awareness and understanding of the conditions around you, so you know exactly what actions to take at what time.

And like in football, it requires a playbook. This playbook.

Of course, you don't run every play in this book all at once and you might not even use all the plays. To succeed in leading from the middle, use the right play in the right situation that's just right for you. The plays will take many forms of specificity: examples, frameworks, checklists, pointed advice, questions to ask, powerful acronyms, and much more. But before you run any plays, let's make sure you understand the field conditions.

Why Is the Middle So Messy?

I asked more than 3,000 managers who lead up, down, and across their organization what the most challenging thing is about their position. Nearly three-quarters of responses had to do with the scope of their responsibility. Within that broad, daunting scope lie five categories of unique difficulties those leading from the middle face, captured in the acronym SCOPE and illustrated in Figure 1.2.

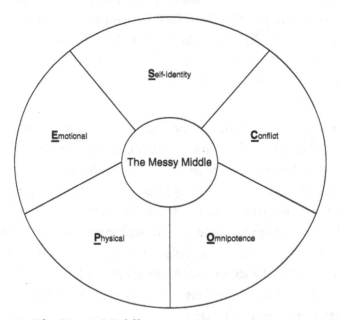

Figure 1.2 The Messy Middle

Leading from the messy middle means dealing with Self-Identity, Conflict, Omnipotence, Physical, and Emotional challenges. Let's first spend time illuminating each of these difficulties, then in the next section you'll get plays to overcome each one.

Self-Identity

When you lead up, down, and across you wear more hats than you can keep track of. It requires constant micro-switching, moving from one role to the other, all day long. (I'll talk more about the expanse of required roles in the "Rock Your Roles" section of this chapter.) One minute you're adopting a deferential stance with your boss, the next you switch into a more assertive mode with your direct reports, then into collaborative mode with your peers. You might switch from moments where you're experiencing tremendous autonomy and a sense of control to moments where you feel like a mere cog in a giant wheel with lots of responsibility but little authority and too little support. You make lots of decisions but maybe not the big, shaping ones. The range of issues and responsibilities is ever broadening, creating still more micro-transitions. Role switching fatigue is exacerbated when you have to perform in front of different levels of management or different functions within one meeting or when you unexpectedly have to jump into one of your roles you weren't mentally prepared to play.

The net result is exhaustion, frustration, and confusion about who you really are and what you should be spending your time doing, which is further exacerbated if you're working in a poorly defined role with unclear expectations and uncertainty about how far your authority extends. And to cap it all off, all the micro-transitions that force you to be spread thin can leave you feeling that while you're certainly busy, you're uncertain of the impact you're really having.

Conflict

When you're surrounded on all sides, it's impossible not to experience conflict. But the leader in the middle has the dubious honor of trying to manage it all. There are natural tensions in the role and pressure that comes from all sides. Your boss cajoles, your employees resist, your peers won't collaborate. You absorb discontent from all around. You deal with conflicting agendas, conflicts of interest, and interpersonal conflicts. If you hear the mantra "more with less" one more time, you might more or less lose it, desperately wanting to counter with "How about we do more with more for once?!" You're inundated with the busywork that comes from being in the middle and being tied to processes and systems and yet you're subject to the time-sucking whims of your chain of command.

You constantly make trade-offs relative to expectations and reconcile priorities with the capacity and talent you have to do the work. You're rewarded for great work with more unexpected work. You're constantly putting out fires but are expected to consistently put up the numbers. You must fiercely compete for and flawlessly allocate resources while fending off those who want more resources from you. You disagree with or didn't have a say in some of the biggest decisions from above and yet have to respond to a lack of understanding and agreement to the direction from below.

Mary Galloway, an Industrial and Organizational Psychologist and faculty member of the Jack Welch Management Institute, told me, "Middle managers are like the middle child of an organization, often neglected by senior managers and blamed by their reports. However, they're still expected to be as charming as the youngest and simultaneously as responsible as the oldest. We end up with middle child syndrome, enshrouded in conflict, wanting more of a say, and not sure how they fit in."

Omnipotence

No one expects frontline, lower-level employees to know everything; they're too inexperienced or too new. Senior managers are excused from this standard because they don't need to know everything, that's what they have their middle managers for. Besides, they make big bets all day, which means big mistakes, which among senior leaders are often seen as a badge of honor.

So where does that leave those who lead from the middle? Like you're expected to know everything, like omnipotence is written into the job description. You have to keep one foot in strategy and the other in day-to-day operations and tactics. You should know your business inside and out and know your competitors just as well. Your market share ticked down in Peoria? You should probably know why. You have to explain the *what*, *how*, and *why* and decide *who*. You must know how to handle the changing nature of work with remote work, global conference calls at ungodly hours, and scads of contracted work the norm. You're expected to know how to grow others despite a lack of investment in you, and without time to grow yourself.

Physical

You've probably heard the term "monkey in the middle." Researchers from Manchester and Liverpool University studied this exact subject, spending 600 hours watching female monkeys in the middle of their hierarchy.[7] They recorded the range of social behavior, including aggressive behavior like threats, chases, and slaps, submissive behaviors like grimacing and retreating, and nurturing behaviors like embracing and grooming. They then measured fecal matter for traces of stress hormones (I'll pass on that duty). They discovered that monkeys in the middle of their hierarchy experienced the most social and physical stress because they deal with the most conflict, you guessed it, up, down, and across their organization. This directly corresponds to what researchers find in the monkeys' slightly brighter cousins, the human beings. In fact, a study of 320,000 employees found that the bottom 5 percent in terms of engagement and happiness levels weren't the people with poor performance ratings or those so new they hadn't moved on yet from an ill-fitting job, but five to ten-year tenured employees in mid-level roles with good performance ratings.[8]

In another big, multi-industry study, researchers from Columbia University and the University of Toronto found that employees in mid-level roles in their organization had much higher rates of depression and anxiety than employees at the top or bottom of the organizational hierarchy. In fact, 18 percent of supervisors and managers experienced symptoms of depression (40 percent said the depression derived from stress), 51 percent of managers were "constantly worried" about work, and 43 percent said the pressure they were under was excessive.[9] Eric Anicich of the University of Southern California's Marshall School of Business says the constant micro-transitions from frequent role changes are psychologically challenging to the point of detriment.[10] For example, disengaging in a high deference task to engage in a high assertiveness task leads to even more stress and anxiety, and a host of related physical problems like hypertension and heart disease.

Emotional

Being in the messy middle means dealing with some unique emotions. It can mean a sense of alienation, isolation, and loneliness, as being in the middle makes it hard to really be a part of anyone's group. Employees can stay at arm's-length, as can bosses, and yet the middle manager attracts and absorbs discontent from every angle, adding to the emotional toll. I've heard many of those who lead from the middle describe feelings of being overworked and underappreciated, expressing great frustration over wanting to change things around them but being unable to do so, not feeling like they can control enough of their destiny. Not to mention that middle managers are often the target of layoffs or can be displaced on the promotion path by outside hires, which can take a huge emotional toll on one's self-esteem and sense of fairness in the world.

A Reframework

While the scope (SCOPE) of what makes leading from the middle so messy can feel daunting, it doesn't have to. Through decades of research and experience I can share with you a framework, or actually a reframework, to help you reframe the way you see, experience, react to, and ultimately resolve each of the specific difficulties outlined. (We'll get into the overall mindset required to thrive as a leader in the middle in the next chapter.) Let's go through the SCOPE acronym again, this time armed with reorienting insights to help reframe and reshape the way you view the inherent, unique difficulties associated with leading from the middle.

Self-Identity

While you're constantly switching roles and changing hats, in flux between high-power and low-power situations, your identity is never actually in flux, even though it might feel like it. An organization is like the human body, it needs a healthy, flexible core. If you strengthen your middle, you strengthen your entire body. If you strengthen the middle of the organization, you strengthen the entire organization. You are the core, flexible center and the center of strength for your company. Take pride in that truth.

Here are some other reframing insights to help you fully appreciate your pivotal place in the organization.

1. You work not in an organization but an organism.   And you're the lifeblood of it.

2. You're the ultimate catalyst from which progress pulses, the amplifier.   We'll cover this in depth in Chapter 3, "The Skillset for Leading Effectively from the Middle."

3. You're the keeper of the long and short-term flame, working on the business and in the business.   This is a unique privilege that those leading from the middle experience.

4. You're a lighthouse and a beacon, signaling threats and drawing all toward opportunities.   It's a powerful duality. For example, being in the middle means you're best suited to spot external threats from competitors and identify internally generated ideas for innovation.

5. The micro-transitions you're constantly making aren't segmented, they're integrated.   The 100 jobs you belong to add up to one vital job you're uniquely suited to do well. Value the variety.

6. While you might be the "middle child," the middle child is also resourceful, creative, and independent.   Galloway reminded me of this, and she's right. These are all things to take pride in.

Conflict

Leading from the middle might be rife with tension, but it also means you're in the thick of things, where the real action is. Your job is to embrace constant contradiction, revel in it, and know that thriving in environments of natural conflict is a valued skill in and of itself. When it comes to environments of conflict, you can shirk, shrink, or shine. Choose the latter to climb the ladder.

More reframing insights follow.

1. You're not squeezed in the middle; you have the unique opportunity to impact in all directions. There's no position quite like it.

2. Instead of getting frustrated that you can't specialize when you're in the middle, which makes it difficult to grow your craft, view the action in the middle as your craft. Redefine success as having mastery over nothing except knowing you must know enough of everything, which takes a special breed to do well.

3. Home builders need permission on everything, business builders don't. So stop asking for permission on everything. Expand your authority within reason. For example, align objectives with your boss upfront, and if your intended action will serve the objective, act, don't ask.

4. Sure, you're in a pressure cooker, but you can release one of the valves—the pressure you put on yourself. If you're focused on constant learning and growth, on becoming a better version of yourself each day and not comparing to others, on chasing authenticity instead of approval, pressure becomes an enabler, not a disabler.

5. Know that ongoing conflict is essential to producing the best work. And you have the opportunity to harness conflict for maximum effect. For instance, I always found that our team produced the best ideas the fastest when we engaged in healthy debate, not when everyone agreed quickly. That's something you can facilitate (you'll get help on that in Chapter 3).

6. The reconciling and reprioritizing habits you're building in the middle (side effects of continually dealing with conflict) will serve you at the top, and everywhere else. More so than any other habits you forge.

Omnipotence

Not knowing can feel like a cardinal sin when you're leading from the middle. But as much as it might feel like it, your job isn't to know everything. In fact, a client I keynoted for had the following sentence painted on the wall in their headquarters lobby: "There's a cost to knowing." It's a reminder to their managers that trying to know everything before moving forward comes at the cost of speed, missed opportunities, and more important priorities neglected elsewhere. For certain, it takes time and resources to know things. Make that known and be aware of the tradeoffs involved for having personal knowledge on a subject. Then, discern if it's worth you personally knowing it. In fact, focus more on discerning what you should know than trying to know everything. Just as important is to build a knowledge system where, if you don't have the answer, you can quickly access someone who will.

Then try the insight-driven plays that follow.

1. Regarding high pressure meetings where you're expected to have all the answers—know what you're truly expected to know, but don't stress out trying to plan for every contingency. Invest the time to prepare for the meeting and anticipate the questions most likely to come up, and be okay with leaning on the knowledge system you've built up for the rest. Ask yourself, "What would the meeting attendees want to know about the subject at hand? What concerns or issues might they have? What are other sources I can have at the ready to answer questions outside my direct realm of expertise?" It's about instilling confidence and an unswerving faith that you and your knowledge system have things covered, not that you personally have the answer to every question.

2. Take pride in what you've chosen not to know. For example, I used to refuse to know some of the smallest details of a project because of the cost of knowing that. I took pride in delegating and empowering others to have the knowledge in certain areas while I focused on knowing enough about that area to be able to ask the right questions and to instill confidence in those evaluating me.

3. Know that it's not about omnipotence, it's about omnipresence. Leaders from the middle should be everywhere in their business, leaving an imprint on virtually everything within their purview (within reason and within boundaries, as I'll discuss in a moment). It requires thoroughly knowing the fundamentals of your business inside and out, but that doesn't come from personally knowing everything. It comes from being present and engaged enough in all aspects of the business (with enough attention to the fundamentals) and by being inclusive and interested enough to engage with all the experts on your business.

Physical

Leading from the middle can most certainly take a physical toll. But you can't take care of everything, or anything, if you don't prioritize taking care of yourself first. That's straight from the playbook of life, let alone this playbook.

Here are a few more reorienting insights to help reduce the physical drains.

1. Know that while you can impact everything, you're not responsible for everything. Period.

2. You're in the middle but aren't at the epicenter of every earthquake.   Not every fire drill needs to be answered. Everyone else's urgent is not your urgent. And acting like it is isn't a good place to be. To illustrate, I can say my most ineffective stint as a middle manager occurred in a role where fire drills constantly sprang up. Instead of filtering them, I fed them, creating a flurry of activity that distracted my organization from more important priorities. Learn from my mistake.

To push back on repeated urgent requests, come from a place of accountability. Meaning, let the requestor know you can't accommodate because of the impact it would have on other critical priorities. Give them a different "yes" by empathetically offering alternatives to you dropping everything. Show them support in other ways.

3. Your physical health and succeeding at work aren't mutually exclusive.   Step out of the grind long enough to realize that. Put your health on a pedestal, the investment will pay dividends personally and professionally. For instance, I find my work gets better the more time I take to work on my health.

4. Be bound by boundaries.   While leading from the middle requires a strong presence everywhere within your scope of responsibility, it doesn't mean your work should cross over into every aspect up, down, and across the organization, and of your life. Boundaries are more important in the middle than anywhere else in an organization because more people have access to you, and so you're disproportionately exposed to stress triggers.

First, give yourself permission to set boundaries. Then, take the time to define what your boundaries are (what you'll engage in, when, within what parameters) and clearly communicate them to others. Pick low-risk situations to practice saying "no" and commit to delegating more. Create structures and processes to help control work and time flow (like agendas), and stick to them. Finally, identify what needs to change to enable your boundaries (like new habits at home that would help keep work at work).

Emotional

It's hard not to get caught up in the emotional strain of being in the middle. But remember that you're part of a pattern. It's not personal, it's a reflection of the position itself.

Here are reframes that speak to the nastiest of the emotional toll—the sense of isolation and being undervalued.

1. It might feel like you're on an island at times, but that can be a good thing.   You're actually a safe haven for workers to express frustrations, voice concerns, share ideas, and take risks without fear of undue punishment. I once took my team to an art studio where each member painted a picture of an island, as a symbolic gesture that *this* team would be an oasis, unlike any other team in the company, a safe-haven and enjoyable place to be, free from typical company nonsense.

At the same time, of course, you also connect to the rest of the organization, and connect disparate parts of the organization to each other, by building bridges.

2. You're not alone, you're on loan, a ninja in the middle, there to make the engine hum.   You're there until your talents elevate you upward in the company or across to something you're more interested in.

3. Senior managers might not always acknowledge your value, but everyone else does.   Recall the earlier Boston Consulting Group research—you're more appreciated than you realize.

4. While at times it might feel like you're not in control of much of anything, you're always in control of your attitude. Just as important, you may have become numb to the amount of daily influence you have in the countless tradeoffs and decisions you make every day. No one in an organization makes more decisions that matter each day than those who lead up, down, and across.

Rock All Your Roles

We talked earlier about the wide variety of roles someone who leads from the middle must take on. My research reveals there are 21 distinct roles middle managers must play. Think of what follows as a 21-gun salute. I'll honor each role with a brief description and then give you plays for each one (I call them "Role Plays"), in the form of the single best piece of advice to succeed with each hat you wear.

1. Translator

A core role of the middle manager is to receive the vision and strategies from above and ensure everyone down (and often across) understands that direction.

The Role Play: Key here is to know that you're not just an explainer, you're an expander. Always add your perspective to upper management directives and help employees understand how their work specifically fits into the broader mission. Give a chance for employees to react to the direction and express concerns (knowing that resistance is often just a cover for wanting to be heard).

2. Converter

Just ensuring everyone understands the direction isn't enough, of course. Middle managers must also convert those visions and strategies into concrete and organized business plans and tactics.

The Role Play: It's critical to do so with an eye on the three *c*'s: competition, capacity, and the customer. Too often I've seen well-intended middle managers develop plans in a silo. They don't consider key competitors' potential reactions, they ignore capacity and try to do far too much while not making enough choices (the easy thing is to do everything), or they fail to truly understand the customer's needs and habits when developing the plans and tactics.

3. Strategist

The best in the middle aren't just tacticians, they also play an active strategic role. No one is closer to changing market dynamics, has more access to new information coming in, or has a closer pulse on what the organization would rally behind. So often I hear, "Strategic thinking is the last thing I have time for" from middle managers. But it should be the first thing you make time for as it impacts every other role you play.

The Role Play: Toggle between the three strategy jobs to do (many mid-level managers stop at the first job). First, cascade top-down strategies to fully implement top management's intentions. Start by fully understanding the strategies, then share perspective to gain commitment when converting the strategies into operational tactics. Second, shape top-down strategies in advance by analyzing information available to you, assessing opportunities and threats, and sharing your perspective and recommendations with decision makers above you. Finally, champion "on the ground" strategies, ones that you and your team create and implement given what you know by being closest to customers, consumers, and competitors. This last strategy job to do is the most often missed or underserved, which is a travesty, as one study showed that a whopping 80 percent of strategic projects initiated by top management failed while 80 percent of those initiated by mid-level managers succeeded.[11]

4. Catalyst

Almost by definition, if you manage up, down, and across, you're
the one who makes things happen. If it is to be, it's up to thee. It's
easy though to get caught up triggering a flurry of activity that's not
necessarily the right activity.

The Role Play: Try the powerful question that follows; I used to ask
myself this as a filter before initiating anything: "Am I about to make
the right thing happen at the right time for the right reason?"

5. Designer

This means designing structures and processes to support
macro-organizational designs.

The Role Play: Don't design in a silo. Enroll the people who will do
the work in the structures and processes you design. What looks good
on paper often doesn't translate in the real world. More structure and
process are not always the answer; the mortal enemy of the Designer is
the Overengineer.

6. Implementor

Sometimes your job is to simply implement someone else's strategies or
plans.

The Role Play: But even then, think about this role not as
order-taking, but as closing the gap between intention and implementation. In other words, fully understand what the strategy or
plan is intended to do, but don't just execute it blindly. To meet that
intent, make adjustments and adaptations along the way based on the
circumstances. While situational leadership is most certainly a thing,
so is situational followership.

7. Decision Maker

All. Day. Long. That's what those in the middle do, make decisions. Key is to ensure you're deciding on the maximum number of things that make the biggest impact.

The Role Play: Negotiate your level of authority to avoid ending up a victim of what researchers call the Karasek model, which says stress is maximized in conditions of high responsibility with little authority to make decisions.[12] Be bold. Get clear on where your decision-making power starts and ends and push the boundaries. Craft an agreement for autonomy with your boss where you spell out the scope of what you get to make the call on and how your boss will be kept up to speed and can input on what you decide.

8. Resource Allocator

Some of the most frequent decisions those who lead from the middle make is how to allocate their resources.

The Role Play: Many things go into good resource allocation, but the most important play is to not underestimate the cost of getting it wrong. For example, poorly allocated resources mean employees are underutilized, projects are delayed, margins drop as more last-minute contractors are hired, and key projects are under-resourced or staffed with the wrong skillsets or equipment. Work as hard and carefully at allocating your resources as you did at obtaining them.

9. Synthesizer

Mid-level managers are at the intersection of the horizontal and vertical information flow in the company; it's easy to get overwhelmed. But the best middle managers avoid analysis paralysis while carefully processing the most important information and using it to trigger action.

The Role Play: The key to being a good synthesizer of information is to listen carefully and be critical of everything you read and hear. The opposite is all too common. For example, it's not unusual to see those leading from the middle take new information and run straight out the window with it because they were in a hurry to decide, because they were overwhelmed with information and just making the call was the easiest way out, or because they weren't skeptical and analytical enough about what was being presented to them. Missteps here also include missing the things not being said or written, failing to keep the motivations in mind of the presenter and getting overly swayed by emotion, and failing to spot discrepancies in data or questionable data sources.

10. Intrapreneur

This refers to taking the initiative to advance innovation, to act like an entrepreneur, within your company.

The Role Play: Deloitte research shows the key to doing this well is to avoid the most common intrapreneurship trap—favoring familiar ideas close in proximity to existing solutions over unfamiliar, new ideas (ones that could result in far more meaningful innovation).[13] This may mean taking calculated risks, breaking some rules, and working "underground" (away from broader scrutiny) with your innovation as long as possible to achieve your goals.

11. Bridge Builder

Everything meets in the middle, by definition. And the middle manager builds the bridges to connect all sorts of groups, up, down, and across the organization to make things happen. Bridges are built and maintained on trust, the subject of many books, so I'll simply laser in on one aspect of this here.

The Role Play: Remember that every action you take will be put by observers (even if subconsciously) into one of two classifications:

something that builds trust or erodes it. Research shows the three best ways to visibly reinforce trust are revealing your thoughts about important issues and encouraging others to raise issues, admitting mistakes, and acting consistently with company values.[14] The opposite of any of these things can destroy the trust you've built up in the blink of an eye. In the middle especially, every action produces a rippling reaction of trust built or broken.

12. Framer

Getting things done from the middle happens by constantly providing context up, down, and across, and by shaping decisions.

The Role Play: Key here is to remember that without proper framing, the building of a house will never progress. Likewise, without proper framing, building support for ideas and desired decisions will never progress, either. So, invest the time it takes to mold and shape the inputs to get the desired outputs. For example, give well-prepared recommendations framed with multiple options and pros and cons for each.

13. Sense Maker

We've established that the middle is messy, which means what passes through it doesn't always make sense. Employees can easily lose the bigger picture and the plot, disconnecting from why they're doing what they're doing and wondering if what they do matters. A big role of the middle manager is to connect employees with the meaning *in* and *at* their work.

The Role Play: As I explain in detail in *Make It Matter*, you create meaning for employees by connecting them to the higher-order purpose behind their work, by feeding their learning and growth, by stoking their sense of competency and self-esteem, by granting autonomy liberally, and by nurturing a caring, authentic, teamwork-based environment. When you help make meaning, you help employees make sense of why they're spending so many hours at their job.

14. Champion

The effective leader in the middle champions ideas they believe in up, down, and across the organization, helping them to fruition.

The Role Play: The key here is to act as an active sponsor, not a passive fan of the initiative. True champions of an initiative or idea roll their sleeves up to help. They bring in allies for support, help overcome detractors, and tout the initiative's benefits while helping identify weaknesses to be shored up. Champions are in a unique position to help an initiative team see around corners and anticipate barriers. Use that power to aid progress.

15. Facilitator

This is about constantly controlling flow, keeping things moving to achieve goals. In the end, no one must be more action-oriented than those who lead from the middle; otherwise you become the bottleneck.

The Role Play: Here's the trick to being a great facilitator, drawn from my experience as a leadership training facilitator. The most important rule of running great training is to design the session with the participants' experience in mind. Think of each opportunity to facilitate in this light. For example, perhaps you're facilitating a meeting between Sales and Product Supply to develop a plan to ship enough product into stores for an upcoming promotion. What does Sales want to experience from the meeting? Put yourself in their shoes. What does Product Supply want to experience? How can you orchestrate the experience of the meeting to produce an outcome that moves things forward?

16. Buffer

Being in the middle means being subject to abruptness and unintended consequences all around. Sometimes you have to scrub and filter messages from others before passing them on, reworking the message to reflect its intent, not its poor execution. Sometimes, a mediator is needed in between parties to keep both sides positive and forward focused. Sometimes a layer is simply needed between the most senior leaders and those below to soften the blow of communications or actions.

The Role Play: Central to being a good buffer is purity of intent. If you have the right intent, you have the right to shape the content. It's not about withholding information or warping truth. It's about carefully molding communications and maintaining a positive culture to help the organization achieve its goals.

17. Straddler

Those in the middle must straddle between long-term objectives and short-term goals, balancing the need to attend to both.

The Role Play: Key here is to not think of the long and short-term as distinct entities. When considering long-term objectives, evaluate current short-term actions to ensure they feed the longer-term objectives. It's easy to lose the plot and chase urgent priorities of the moment that are, in truth, inconsistent with achieving a long-term objective. And when engaged in short-term activities, pay attention to what you learn along the way and let it inform and inspire the formulation of long-term objectives.

18. Accountability Czar

Fostering a sense of accountability isn't just about holding your employees accountable. It starts with you acting like an owner and holding yourself accountable, as well as holding senior managers accountable.

The Role Play: Author Peter Bregman has the essence of driving accountability exactly right—it's about achieving clarity on five things. Be clear on expectations, capability (resources and skills required to complete the work), measurement, feedback, and consequences.[15] It's as simple as that, but know that it's an all-or-nothing proposition. If you miss on any one of these five points, accountability will crumble.

19. Communicator, 20. Coach, 21. Team Builder

Each of these vital roles will be covered in depth in Chapters 3, 5, and 6, respectively.

Those who lead from the middle experience a breadth and depth of scope and roles like no one else in an organization. Revel in the choreographed dance you excel at. Believe that leading effectively from the middle is a craft and that you're on your way to becoming a craft master, something to take pride in. Know that you don't have to be *the* leader to be *a* leader. Realize that you're the center of progress, that you exist to make a profound impact and to infuse your workplace with energy and a winning attitude. Believe that you're a tour de force and attack your scope and roles with passion, fueled now by power plays for each scope and role challenge.

Know that leading successfully from the middle is also a mindset and a skillset. So, set your mind now to Chapter 2, where we open the playbook to learn the mindset required.

Notes:

1. P. Evans, "Management 21C," Chapter 5, *Financial Times*, Prentice Hall (2000), in *Emerging Leadership: A Handbook for Middle Manager Development* (IDeA).

2. "Why Middle Managers May Be the Most Important People in Your Company," knowledge.wharton.upenn.edu (May 25, 2011).

3. B. Snyder, "Researchers: How Much Difference Does a Boss Make?" gsb.stanford.edu (September 27, 2012).

4. "The Middle Revolution," tinypulse.com.

5. J. Caye et al., "Creating a New Deal for Middle Managers," The Boston Consulting Group (July 2010).

6. J. Gehman, "Where Are They Now: Marty Lyons," newyorkjets.com (November 8, 2018).

7. "Monkey Study Reveals Why Middle Managers Suffer the Most Stress," manchester.ac.uk (April 2013).

8. J. Zenger and J. Folkman, "Why Middle Managers Are So Unhappy," *Harvard Business Review*, hbr.org (November 2014).

9. S. Prins, L.M. Bates, K.M. Keyes, and C. Muntaner, "Anxious? Depressed? You Might Be Suffering from Capitalism: Contradictory Class Locations and the Prevalence of Depression and Anxiety in the USA," onlinelibrary.wiley.com (August 2015).

10. E. Anicich and J. Hirsh, "Why Being a Middle Manager Is So Exhausting," *Harvard Business Review*, hbr.org (March 2017).

11. Q. Huy, "In Praise of Middle Managers," *Harvard Business Review*, hbr .org (September 2001).

12. J. Kain and S. Jex, "Karasek's (1979) Job Demands-Control Model: A Summary of Current Issues and Recommendations for Future Research," emerald.com (March 2010).

13. "Five Insights into Entrepreneurship," www2.deloitte.com (2015).

14. S. Rock and M. Rock, "The Middle Manager Lifeline," Think Publishing (September 2016).

15. P. Bregman, "The Right Way to Hold People Accountable," *Harvard Business Review*, hbr.org (January 2016).

2 The Mindset for Leading Effectively from the Middle

T he mental approach required to be a successful manager from the middle is unlike any other in the field of leadership. With daily exposure to such a wide range of employees, peers, and bosses with so many individual wants, needs, problems, aspirations, and insecurities, and so many hats to be worn (as you saw in Chapter 1), a different mindset is a must. I'm excited to offer you just that, a powerful mindset born from decades of research and experience and discerned from other mental approaches for its consideration of the unique conditions those who lead from the middle must operate in.

The Others-Oriented Leadership Mindset

The most effective mindset for leading from the middle is what I call the "others-oriented" leadership mindset, named as such because it takes the focus off of self and places it on understanding and acting on the multitude of perspectives you must consider when interacting up, down, and across your organization. If you want to thrive in leading from the middle, it can't be all about you. It's about helping everyone and everything around you to thrive. It's about the ecosystem, not the ego system.

For this reason, others-oriented leadership is related to servant leadership; it's even from the same leadership tree. However, it's a different branch with critical differences.

Classical servant leadership invokes an inverted leadership hierarchy; that is, the leader's main function is to serve those below him or her, putting employees' needs first, rather than vice versa. You don't think less of yourself; you just think of yourself less. You know that strength doesn't make you capable of rule, it makes you capable of service.

But service doesn't mean subservience.

With others-oriented leadership, while power flows through you in servitude, you don't deny your power, knowing when it must flow from you. You lead with others in mind, but make no mistake, you serve *and* you lead—you don't lose your authoritative leadership qualities, which can happen with a pure servant leadership mindset. You know when it's time to command and direct versus support and stay in the shadows.

Others-oriented leadership further distinguishes itself from classic servant leadership by avoiding the five stigmas (whether they're fair or not) associated with servant leadership.

1. Servant leaders can be pegged as too "soft."

In fact, the man who coined and popularized the term "servant leadership," Robert Greenleaf, said the best test of whether or not you're a servant leader is, "Do those served grow as persons?"[1] Others-oriented leadership adds a second primary test, "Does the business grow?" In other words, others-oriented leaders ensure it's understood they value results, and how those results are achieved, equally. It means they spend as much time and energy on planning and executing to achieve company goals as helping individuals achieve theirs. They recognize at times they must first serve what the business needs, not what the people want. They know that what's needed for the business and/or employees doesn't always feel good. But despite the tension, they proceed with deliberateness, and always with empathy. They think like an engineer, feel like an artist.[2]

2. Servant leaders can fail to establish their authority and mastery.

As mentioned previously, in an effort to serve, servant leaders can over-abdicate authority and fade into the woodwork, at times becoming invisible to the organization as to their impact. They might take refuge in the comfort of serving their employees, not wanting to engage up the chain as much (which can be the opposite of comforting) and thus not establishing as strong a presence with their leaders.

All organizations love servant leaders, but they also want to know those leaders are highly competent leaders in their own right, with authority, control, and the ability to influence in all directions. Others-oriented leadership calls for a careful balance between stepping back to lead from behind and stepping up to lead from the front. Guidance for how to strike the right balance is coming up later in this chapter, in the "What's a Given" section.

3. Servant leaders can struggle with authoritative, command and control–type leaders.

Leading from the middle by definition means you must be effective upward. And yet, classic servant leaders often run into conflict with bosses who don't share the same leadership philosophies. For example, priorities can quickly clash with the servant leader seeking to protect the people first, and their leader wanting to protect profit first.

And related to number two above, the boss might want to see their subordinates with a servant leader style more clearly distinguish themselves from followers, believing that the servant leader style sacrifices the establishment of authority and mastery. This can chip away at the servant leader's credibility in the eyes of their boss, making it more difficult for that servant leader to get the resources and support needed to best serve their constituents. I've personally experienced this. Net, having an others-oriented leadership mindset helps those with a servant heart maintain that spirit, while upping their game in managing up. By the way, Chapter 4 ("Leading Your Boss") gives you the specific playbook for taking your leading up skills to a new level.

4. Servant leaders can be too one-dimensional in where their energy goes.

In their zeal to serve subordinates, they can underserve their chain of command, peers, and even underserve themselves. Reports of compassion fatigue (getting burned out in trying to always put others' needs first) are not uncommon with servant leaders. With others-oriented leadership, it's about directing energy and focus in every direction, up, down, and across the organization, not just downward—and yes, not forgetting to serve yourself as well.

5. Servant leadership doesn't fit every situation.

For example, in times of change (which we'll cover in Chapter 8, "Leading Change") or in times of crisis, a more authoritative approach is required. Or in the case of a leader working with new, young teams who may not know what to ask for, what help looks like, or what to do, servant leadership per se isn't the best fit. The mix of servitude and authoritativeness in the others-oriented leadership mindset is more flexible, applicable to any situation middle managers face.

The bottom line is that there are important aspects of leading and influencing up, down, and across that can't all best be handled with a blanket servant leader approach. Let's get into more specifics about what others-oriented leadership entails and how you can specifically embody it. What follows is a tool I've been teaching others for years; it will help you consistently practice the others-oriented leadership mindset.

The Others-Oriented Compass

When working from the frenzied middle it can be easy to retreat into yourself, to grasp onto self-interest as an anchor and lose sight of those around you whom you're trying to influence and serve. This tool will help you keep your orientation outwardly focused.

First, know that the others-oriented leadership mindset boils down to four considerations: what you give, what you give up, what's a given, and what you get. The topline detail for these considerations is crisply provided in the diagram in Figure 2.1, meant to visually reflect a compass, a tool to help you stay on course. (I carried a picture of this tool in my wallet to remind me how to act as an others-oriented

Figure 2.1 The Others-Oriented Compass

leader.) Below the diagram you'll find an explanation for each aspect of the others-oriented leadership mindset, and in keeping with the compass theme, specific direction for bringing each aspect to life.

What You Give

If you're operating with an others-oriented leadership mindset, you give:

1. Credit and praise. I learned long ago as a leader that the more credit and praise you give away, the more that comes back. This includes finding genuine reasons to praise your boss (balanced with corrective feedback, as we'll talk about in Chapter 4), getting that same balance right with your employees (as we'll discuss in Chapter 5), and bragging about your peers to their boss (as we'll cover in Chapter 6). Employees in all directions are starved for appreciation. In a survey I conducted among 3,000 executives, a whopping 68 percent felt underappreciated. Being a leader in the middle puts you in a unique position to create a positive ripple effect of gratitude.

The truth is, managers tend to give praise as much as they get praised (or not), up, down, and across the chain. Being stingy with credit and praise only encourages others to be the same way—not the multiplier effect you want.

Specific direction: Be frequent but not frivolous with praise, making sure to tie it to results or any other stated goal, or it will feel superfluous and disingenuous. And deliberate how you deliver the praise, personalizing it so you don't trivialize it. If you give generic praise for the same things to everyone in the same way, it loses its meaning. Take the time to think through how to tailor the praise to the individual and how they like to receive praise.

2. Informed encouragement. This is a special brand of encouragement that you're best suited to provide, given your access to perspective from all directions. In other words, you can hearten others and provide affirmation with specific reasons and rationale you have access to as a mid-level manager. You can back up your optimism (as opposed to just rash cheerleading), which makes it more meaningful.

For example, you can explain to employees why there's reason for hope in times of adversity based on detailed plans you've heard from your bosses. You can bolster upper management's excitement about why a plan will work based on perspective you uniquely have from frontline employees. You can encourage peers based on your access to the overall big picture that you're given.

And not to be lost, as a leader from the middle it's critical that you think of yourself as the epicenter of encouragement. In my 3,000-executive survey I asked: "In the past six months has anything happened at work that's caused you to take a step back in your self-confidence?" 93 percent said yes. The people all around you need your inspiration more than you know.

I believe affirmation is one of the most powerful forces on earth. And I believe that it takes multiple volts of positivity from a leader to overcome one volt of negativity. Employees are far more likely to absorb and obsess on negative inputs than positive ones (true for you, too, no?). In fact, research shows we're four times more likely to remember criticism than we are praise. Negativity can fester and spread far more quickly, deeply, and broadly than optimism does, so don't assume an occasional dose of encouragement is enough. Be the epicenter of positivity.

Specific direction: Here are two simple but very powerful ways to make your encouragement more meaningful and resonant. Before giving your next dose of encouragement, pause and ask this one-word question: "Why?" Meaning, why should your audience be encouraged by your words? What is the detailed reason behind it or what information or perspective can you share that lends it credibility?

There's nothing wrong with a "You can do it!" but it's far more powerful when they understand specifically *why* they can do it.

Try this as well. Ask employees what their goals are. Then validate those goals out loud. You'll be amazed at how motivating your verbal stamp of approval can be. Offer your partnership in helping them achieve that goal to really ramp up the encouragement.

3. Bedrock respect.   Yes, all leaders should remember to give respect, but for others-oriented leaders, it's a foundational, bedrock behavior. Visible respect for the other with every interaction at every level. No exceptions. It's about believing that everyone is valued and valuable, worthy and worthwhile. Sadly, such behavior will actually stand out; research shows a stunning 90 percent of employees believe that basic workplace civility is a problem.[3] So consistently being respectful to others will earn you respect right back.

Specific direction: To keep your respect quotient toward others high, try this powerful mental daily habit. Right before engaging with someone, ask yourself, "How will I act in this interaction?" Try it for the next 10 people you engage with. It will dramatically alter the quality of each engagement, especially for those you might struggle with on a personal level. Stick to it and it will soon become a routine for respect.

4. Your time and full attention.   When you lead from the middle, it's important to understand that much of your time is not yours. The job *is* to give of your time and to do your work through others. The trick is to expend energy up, down, and across without underserving in any one direction. Just being mindful of the fact that you lie in the middle, with people all around you who could benefit greatly from your energy and effort, *and that it's what you're there for*, is a huge part of it.

You can send the signal that you're open for the business of helping in all directions by simply showing warmth, an interest in others' well-being, and a desire to connect. Or by rolling up your sleeves and helping someone with a circumstance. And remember, when-in, be all-in, meaning, be fully present with others. That time you were looking at your phone while meeting with someone or when you seemed mentally elsewhere will be the time they disproportionately remember.

Specific direction: Take the time for others, especially when you think you don't have it. They'll notice. Odds are when you really don't have the time, you're in the middle of something important that involves many of those around you who likely also don't have lots of time. The fact that you took the time for them, even when time-pressed, won't go unnoticed and will send a clear signal of the depth of your others-orientation.

Note that I'm not saying sacrifice every minute of every day to be available, or don't block off time when you need to. I'm talking about those marginal moments in between where you can choose to engage with others or not. Default to the former. And when with others, remind yourself to be mindful, not mind full. If you catch yourself mentally drifting, simply ask, "What has my attention right now?"

5. Unswerving support and empowerment. Others-oriented leaders in the middle are the Grand Central Station for providing the resources, structure, processes, coaching, and guidance needed to help the organization around them thrive. So many desired destinations (goals to be achieved) flow through you—take pride in that. As you do, equip your employees to operate with freedom and autonomy, empowered to achieve objectives as they see fit, with your steady hand at the ready. This means doing the hard work of giving away work: agreeing to the objectives and scope of their autonomy and the work to be done and defining corresponding success measures. It means explaining the *why* instead of dictating the *how*, setting employees up to win with the resources and training they need, then letting them do what they were hired to do while checking-in from time to time (versus just checking out). It also means tearing down roadblocks and intervening when employees and their projects are in harm's way, with the zeal of a mother bear protecting her cubs. And it means providing access to contacts, networks, and opportunities to help them achieve their goals (both professional and personal).

Specific direction: You'll get lots of direction on how to effectively coach your employees in Chapter 5. In terms of providing unswerving support and empowerment, for now, write down the sentence that follows in all-caps at the top of every meeting agenda or on a note card to tape to your office wall, cubicle wall, or home-office wall. It's the golden question others-oriented leaders should constantly ask themselves regarding their daily work:

AM I ASSISTING SUCCESS OR AVOIDING FAILURE?

Think about it. If you act like you're assisting success, you're living the core role of the leader from the middle in terms of providing unswerving support and empowerment.

But if you're avoiding failure, your actions look different. You micromanage. You're indecisive. You ask for too many reports, studies, or focus groups to test and retest and cover your butt. You're too conservative and unwilling to take risks. You aren't proactive and forward thinking. You spend way too much time crafting careful explanations and communications up the chain and ask for way too little support and resources for down the chain. All of this is not playing the role of a catalyst, but of guarding against a cataclysm. If you catch yourself engaged in avoiding failure behaviors versus assisting success behaviors, follow the one-sentence direction above to change course.

6. Assurance of mastery.   In their zest to serve, empower, and focus on their people, those with a servant's heart can sometimes distance themselves from day-to-day operations and lose sight of the need to have and demonstrate a deep understanding of their business. You may feel tension between spending time on, with, and for your people versus spending it on analysis or sharpening your business acumen. Balance is key.

As mentioned in Chapter 1 and as we'll touch upon again in Chapter 4 ("Leading Your Boss"), the balance starts with spending enough time on the fundamentals of your business. This includes preparing for meetings with your chain of command where you can demonstrate mastery of your business (while still shining a spotlight on your team) and can show you're providing compelling direction. The harsh truth is you can't serve your organization if your leaders don't think you're fit to serve your business.

Balance between your people and your business also means that while you liberally grant autonomy, once again, you stay involved enough in the details of the key drivers of your business to know if you're on track or not, why, and what needs to be done to course correct if needed. It means staying close enough to your customers and consumers to know what their wants and needs are and how well you're fulfilling those. It means digging into data to gain a personal understanding of what's happening in your business.

The skeptic might say, but isn't all of this the opposite of being others-oriented; that is, focusing on demonstrating what I can do and the knowledge/knowledge systems I have? Remember, the others-oriented leadership mindset is about understanding and acting on the unique perspective of everyone up, down, and across. It most often requires a mindset of servitude, but at times, you must establish your authority and mastery. The "up" part of up, down, and across, in particular, needs to know that you know your business. When they do, you're working from a much better place to confidently serve down and across.

Assurance of mastery also means ensuring that everyone you work with feels like they're part of a high-achieving, championship team—a unit that shows mastery in their craft to accomplish big results. That happens when, at the end of the day, you get results. So, think of this as a reminder that as a leader in the middle you must hold yourself and those around you to the highest level of accountability to hit your objectives. It's one of the best ways you can serve others.

Specific direction: Do a weekly "COO Check." It's a potent trick I used every Friday. If you're operating with an others-oriented leadership mindset, you're already acting like a CSO (Chief Servant Officer or Chief Support Officer if you like). Every Friday, review your activity and progress for that week, then ask yourself if you could represent yourself as the Chief Operating Officer of your business. In other words, while granting autonomy, coaching, providing resources, removing roadblocks, and all the "servant stuff," have you stayed close enough to the nitty gritty operations of your business, the key drivers of what makes your business flounder or flourish? A COO would say "yes," and leading from the middle means being part COO. If your answer is "no," the next week be mindful about spending enough time getting as close to your business as you do getting close to your people.

What You Give Up

If you're an others-oriented leader, you give up:

1. Self-interest as first priority. This is inherent in effectively leading from the middle given the unique opportunity for you to help, support, and serve in all directions to grow the people and the business. But given the constant demands and pulls you experience from all directions, compassion fatigue (mentioned earlier) can kick-in where you burn out on serving everyone else's needs and ignore your own. It's a natural, human response that can develop and that can be avoided. Help follows below.

Specific direction: The key is maintaining balance and staying steadfast in making it not about you while not losing yourself entirely in the name of servitude. To help get the balance right, first, don't think of self-interest and the interest of others as mutually exclusive. By enthusiastically embracing your role in the middle with a servant's heart, it will flow back to benefit you immensely as your reputation as an others-oriented leader (one whom everyone wants to work for and with) grows. Remembering this should make it easier for you to hold steady in your commitment to deprioritize your self-interest in your day-to-day actions.

That said, introduce a third test of the others-oriented leadership mindset, along with "Do those served grow as persons?" and "Does the business grow?" And that is, "Are *you* growing?" This means ensuring along the way that you're taking time for your own personal growth, development, and well-being. For example, one successful middle manager I know creates an annual personal learning, health, and development plan for himself each January. He then enrolls his boss on the plan to help him stay accountable for sticking to it. He doesn't deprioritize others and everything else to achieve completion of the plan, he simply considers it an important "and."

2. Power and control (selectively).   When you're an others-oriented leader, by definition, giving up power and control is the obvious part. Doing so selectively is the key, which is trickier. It starts with understanding that power flows through you, not from you, for the most part. That's part of the deal if you want to lead effectively from the middle. This includes generally abdicating sole decision-making power, opting instead to actively enroll key stakeholders in the decision-making process. It means listening to others before deciding instead of wanting others to listen to you when it's time to decide. It's about leaning on personal power more than position power to make things happen.

That said, as touched upon earlier, you still must be mindful of showing up as authoritative and exercising control when it's called for. What follows is help for getting that right.

Specific direction: Exercising power and control selectively is all about spotting those authoritative moments of truth, those times when you best serve yourself (and your organization) by taking on a more traditional "command and control" role. To identify those moments, ask yourself this simple but illuminating question: "When does my boss (or the organization) need to know that I know?" Meaning, when is it important to show up as being in command of the details, as having a solid strategic and tactical plan, as being in control? It's in those moments that you reassert yourself. For example, say your competitor just made a surprising, aggressive move in the marketplace that could mean substantial harm to your business. It's safe to say your boss and your organization need to know soon thereafter that you know what to do and have a plan accordingly.

3. The limelight (selectively).   The first two words in "others-oriented leadership" are a dead giveaway that you give up the spotlight, opting instead to put it on your people and their accomplishments. Again, though, up to a point. The specific direction I offer here ties closely to that for giving up power and control selectively (described above).

Specific direction: Others-oriented leaders lift as they climb, but not always in the shadow of the mountain. Meaning, as you rise up the organization, you're naturally focused on bringing others along with you, helping them to learn, grow, and develop their potential, as you are. Most often as you're climbing up that company mountain (hierarchy), it's done quietly, in the shadows, with you not asking for or adding to the fanfare. But in those times when you must show up as authoritative and exercise your power and control (as discussed previously), it will cast the limelight on you, by definition. In those moments it's all about remembering the "we" and not drifting to "I."

For example, say you're presenting important new strategies and tactics to your organization at an annual meeting. Say "we" much more than "I." In this way, you're accepting the limelight, but under your own terms and conditions.

4. Information.   It's hard enough to compete effectively against competitors in today's business world when you have full information, so why in the world would you withhold information from your people? And yet, classical command-and-control leaders often do that. They hold information close to the vest as a way to maintain power and control, even to manipulate. Those operating with an others-oriented leadership mindset openly share information to foster and feed a knowledge-sharing culture.

Specific direction: Think of information sharing as an investment, not an intrusion. Taking the time to share information makes a huge difference in the actual performance of your employees as well as feeds the vibe of openness, transparency, and a sense of community. It's one of the primary tools you have for getting work done through others. Your efforts on this front will be noticed and appreciated and will likely differentiate you from other leaders as well. The key is to allot sufficient time for the work required in sharing information properly. It requires constant communication, context, and framing when you do. Leaders often shy away from information sharing because it's just easier not to. It's an understandable temptation, but one that others-oriented leaders avoid.

It's also important to note there are certainly times when you must hold information close to the vest (like knowledge of a pending divestiture for which no details have been provided, etc.). This is about living the general spirit of sharing versus shirking your responsibility to do so.

5. Hubris and ego.   Again, apparent in the words "others-oriented" is the fact that your arrogance and vanity are not drivers of your actions.

Such things should be replaced with humility and vulnerability. It means that even though when leading from the middle you're surrounded by others who need you, that doesn't mean you have to be the smartest person in the room all the time. You become smarter and create a smarter organization by leveraging the collective talent of the whole. You become smarter by admitting what you don't know. The problem is, while we intuitively know the importance of showing vulnerability as a leader (for the humanity it shows, the trust it builds, and the emotional connection it makes), how to show up vulnerable as a leader is less obvious. Here's help.

Specific direction: The key here is to do the easy and hard stuff in giving up hubris and ego. Others-oriented leaders naturally don't seek credit, pointing at others with success and in the mirror with failures. The hard stuff is to be brave and step up in settings that will "expose" you, like big town hall meetings or key team gatherings. Let your organization see themselves in you. Admit mistakes, faults, struggles, or that you don't have all the answers. Your admitted imperfections will validate to employees that it's okay they have them, too. Think about it as confiding in your organization, asking for and accepting help, and accepting that self-doubt is a part of leadership. Of course, no one is asking you to empty all the skeletons in your closet. Vulnerability as a leader is sharing what will be of service to the organization.

6. The need to be liked all the time. It's a mathematical impossibility when leading from the middle to be liked by everyone all the time. There are just too many interactions and permutations. By no means am I saying don't try to be more likable; research shows when you are you have greater sway over others.[4] In fact, you can boost your likeability quotient significantly by simply keeping in mind what I call the Fondness Four: 1. Focus on being interested, not interesting, 2. Open up and invite others in, 3. Pass up opportunities to pass judgment, 4. Don't get sucked into an orbit of negativity.

The bigger point here is that despite all your best efforts, tension is inevitable. Period. And yet, those with a servant's heart can get caught up chasing approval instead of authenticity. It gets most troublesome when the leader alters who they genuinely are to curry constant favor from those all around. It's an empty victory at best when you win approval of someone you were seeking it from and a soul-crushing pursuit at worst. I learned that firsthand because not only did I hate the thought of not being liked, even by just one person, I didn't even like someone not liking the outcome of a meeting with me.

The reality is that leading from the middle means you have to make tough calls at times that some won't like, and you'll have to move quickly in ways that sometimes people will take unintended offense to.

Specific direction: Keep purity of intent on a pedestal. This worked magic for me. It means to always keep in front of you, and hold in the highest regard, what your honest intent is with your words or actions. If it's pure and well-intended, then you've done what you can do and can't worry about what others think of you. Sure, you can keep working at minimizing misinterpretation by being mindful of what you say, how you say it, and what your actions are (to ensure it all matches your intent). But if you consistently come from a place of good intent, remind yourself of that and don't look back. And know that consistently having purity of intent is something people will notice over time, which will buy you leeway and the benefit of the doubt in those times when your words and actions don't sit right with someone, which is inevitable when leading from the middle.

What's a Given

If you're acting with an others-oriented leadership mindset, these things are a given:

1. Concern for success of all stakeholders. This of course means leading with others in mind, with concern for their success over

your sole self-interest. Concern includes caring and empathy, and stakeholders include shareholders—which is a reminder that others-oriented leaders care about delivering results as much as they care about those who deliver the results.

Specific direction: Conduct periodic organizational health surveys. Stay close to not only the results the organization is producing, but how they're feeling along the way and whether or not they're achieving their individual goals.

2. You ask and act. This is related to the above but worthy of its own mention. Being others-oriented means staying in touch with others, which you do by inquiring. Care enough to ask questions of your organization to assess needs, concerns, and emotions. Ask for feedback and what you can do to help. Then act on that input. Asking but not acting on the input is far more damaging than not asking at all. I see this happening all the time with leadership teams that survey and interview employees, then bury or never share the findings, let alone take action on them. Poison.

Specific direction: Remember this quote from Mary Kay Ash, founder of Mary Kay Cosmetics: "Everyone has an invisible sign hanging from their neck saying, 'Make me feel important.'"[5] The point isn't to be patronizing but to remember that people want to know you value engaging with them and respect what they say enough to act on it.

3. Willingness to share a prioritized workload. When employees see you rolling up your sleeves to help with their work, it reminds them that you're one of them, and that you're not above the work that gets done below. Helping peers in this manner displays a communal "flow to the work" vibe. To bosses it looks like initiative. All as long as it's work that's been consciously chosen for its connection to advancing a stated objective or goal.

Specific direction: Roll up your sleeves to help as a visible gesture, not as "I'll do it myself" behavior. And remind yourself that the easy thing is to do everything. Prioritizing and making tough choices isn't easy but it's another powerful way to serve your organization. Two tricks to help with this. First, strive for 20/20 vision, meaning, continually be evaluating the most important 20 percent of work to stay focused on it, until it's time to shift to the next most important 20 percent. Below that, the work probably isn't a true priority. Second, have a "To Do" list and a "To Don't" list. It drives awareness of the kind of non-priority work that tends to pop up that you don't want to get sucked into.

4. Prioritizing investment in others.   Others-oriented leaders focus on developing new leaders, not new followers. They act as the soil, not the sun. The sun shines down from on high with intense heat and an inescapability that can lead to scorched earth. The soil provides a warm, nurturing environment that surrounds and helps spur growth.

Specific direction: You are, at least in part, your results. But also judge how good you are based on how good your employees have become. Ask yourself this simple question as a test: Are you as passionate about the growth, development, and career of your employees and peers as you are about your own? If so, work with them to develop learning, growth, and career plans. If not, acknowledge it, own it, and open up to the purest joy of others-oriented leadership—helping others become better versions of themselves.

5. Readiness to flex to authoritative mode.   This speaks to the core of what distinguishes others-oriented leadership from its close cousin, servant leadership. It's about being mindful of when to flex your authoritative muscle and building your skills to do so, especially in terms of leading the most difficult other—your chain of command (again, covered in Chapter 4, "Leading Your Boss"). It can be difficult to switch into authoritative mode, but it's a necessary tension to maintain. I'm not suggesting that you shift your focus to building empires over empathy or to embody power versus empower. It's about shifting gears a bit when the engine calls for it.

Specific direction: We talked earlier in this chapter about spotting those authoritative moments of truth. Also know that authoritative mode is about being assertive versus aggressive. Aggressive behavior is disruptive, overbearing, disregards others, is defensive, and serves to intimidate. Assertive behavior is standing up for your ideas and beliefs, clearly articulating and defending them, directly and visibly communicating to key stakeholders, and putting strong self-confidence on display. It's about respecting boundaries and others' viewpoints while still protecting needs and advancing agendas. Create reminders for yourself on the importance between the two. For example, before any critical team meeting or big meeting with upper management, I'd write four words at the top of the meeting agenda as a reminder: "Be assertive, not aggressive."

6. Everything from authenticity.   All your actions should come from the root of *who* you are and *how* you are. Operate with openness and honesty, vulnerability, humility, and a genuine desire to serve. Draw others to you based on your character, not your personality.

Specific direction: Remember these two things. First, nothing is more transparent than when people aren't being transparent. Second, leading from the middle gives you the right to make all kinds of mistakes. But you can never make mistakes of motive.

What You Get

If you're an others-oriented leader, you get many positive benefits in return. If you're not getting the things below, it should set off an alarm, indicating that you may need to adjust your mindset to be more others-oriented. In this section, I'll give one piece of specific direction at the end.

1. Trust and loyalty. When you give trust and loyally serve, it's the very first thing you should get back.

2. Full engagement. Gallup has identified 12 questions that serve as the leading indicators of whether or not an employee is fully engaged.[6] Eight of those questions involve others-oriented aspects of leadership. For example, "In the last seven days, have I received recognition or praise for doing good work?," "Does my supervisor, or someone at work, seem to care about me as a person?," "Is there someone at work who encourages my development?," and "Do I know what's expected of me at work?" You get the idea. You should be seeing commitment, not mere compliance, if you're others-oriented enough.

3. Sense of community and kinship. The service mindset inherent in others-oriented leadership is so powerful, research shows it creates a trickle-down effect, spreading servant-like behaviors up, down, and around the organization.[7] Feelings of community and kinship soon follow.

4. Accountability. Related to the above, accountability is further enhanced by a sense of mutual interdependence, which is further fueled by a sense of community and kinship. Prevalence of blame dodging and excuses in an organization may be an indication that the leader is role-modeling too much self-orientation versus others-orientation.

5. Strength in adversity/resilience. In tough times we lean on each other. Does your organization become more cohesive or divisive in such times? You should be seeing far more of the former if you're fully operating as an others-oriented leader.

6. Peak performance.   An others-oriented leadership mindset leads to peak performance because it blends a focus on achieving results with how those results are achieved, that is, with an empathetic eye toward others (which makes the results far more sustainable by the way). Thus, if business isn't responding the way you want, it's likely your people aren't either.

Specific direction: You won't know what you're getting without paying close attention to what your organization is giving. With all that requires your attention when leading from the middle, you need help in assessing this. So put a key tracking mechanism in place—reverse mentors. Ask a few people you've developed a particularly strong relationship with lower in the organization to serve as your mentor in reverse, giving you honest feedback and observations about how the surrounding organization is delivering on the six "What You Gets." If a sense of community or accountability, for example, is lacking, the reverse mentor can help raise awareness of that and help illuminate why. Those lower in the organization than you will have a valuable, unfiltered perspective to share.

So, the Others-Oriented Compass is intended to keep you on course, pointing you toward the right mindset to act on. In Chapter 3, we move from mindset to skillset.

Notes:

1. "What Is Servant Leadership?" Center for Servant Leadership, greenleaf .org.

2. S. Prichard, "How Servant Leaders Achieve Better Results," skiprichard .com (September 2017).

3. J. Dutton, "Fostering High Quality Connections," *Stanford Social Innovation Review*, ssir.org (Winter 2003).

4. "Scientifically Proven Ways to Become More Influential," Hoffeld Group, hoffeldgroup.com.

5. A. Meah, "35 Inspirational Mary Kay Ash Quotes on Success," awakenthegreatnesswithin.com.

6. "The Gallup Q12 Employee Engagement Questionnaire," SHRM, shrm .org (May 1, 2010).

7. D. Melchar and S. Bosco, "Achieving High Organization Performance through Servant Leadership," *The Journal of Business Inquiry* 9 (1): 74–88 (2010).

3 The Skillset for Leading Effectively from the Middle

There are so many roles to play and so many things for an effective, others-oriented leader from the middle to think about. But what's the net spirit and essence of all the activity the successful middle manager engages in? Into what role do all other roles feed at the highest level? What's the highest-level skill required, and the skillset required to succeed within?

I wanted to pinpoint this, so I interviewed or surveyed 1,000 others-oriented leaders leading from the middle. I asked them to step back and describe their job when it was being done at its best. Very clear themes emerged. In fact, I kept hearing one word in particular, over and over.

Amplify.

Those who lead from the middle with an others-oriented mindset and do it well describe their job on the whole as being an amplifier. You're not a mere conduit between everything and everyone up, down, and across. You make things that need to be heard, heard. You make things clearer and more powerful—like an amplifier. You bring the micro to the macro. You bring a quality to what people hear by sharing your perspective and framing it properly. You amplify the strengths of your employees and peers by investing heavily in them, amplify senior leadership's vision, mission, and strategies (making sure they connect to the team's daily work), amplify the team's effectiveness and output, and amplify the entire organization's capabilities and results. You share and amplify the truth, data, and different perspectives, in all directions.

Amplifying is not order-taking. Sometimes you amplify someone else's signal, sometimes you're the source of the original signal (for example, you might create the strategies)—but the successful, others-oriented leader in the middle is always amplifying something in some context. And the amplifier essence is not something to feel like you're being relegated to, but elevated to.

So, what of the core skills required to succeed as an amplifier? Seven skills in particular clearly emerged from research, breaking out from the pack for the frequency in which they were brought up as success drivers. And as luck would have it, I can offer the perfect seven-letter acronym to help you remember each skill: AMPLIFY. The acronym is spelled out below, then we'll tackle each skill/letter one at a time for the rest of the chapter.

Adaptability

Meshing

Political savviness

Locking in

Influencing

Fostering compromise

You setting the tone

Adaptability

Mid-level managers must learn to adapt simply because they live in the middle of chaos. Ever changing (even competing) priorities, requests, directives, objectives, and marketplace dynamics are just a few of the elements in constant flux. You have to be like the flexible section of those two-part "bendy buses" you see every now and then, accommodating the rigidities of the vehicle while ensuring the front and back are moving in the same direction. No easy task, this adapting. But know that great adaptability comes from three types of flexibility in particular.

First, intellectual flexibility, which requires keeping an open mind, incorporating new data and drawing conclusions accordingly, switching quickly back and forth between the big picture and detail, creative solutioning, and leveraging your learning agility (ability to learn).

Next is emotional flexibility. Specifically, not getting overly emotional about changing conditions in a way that negatively influences behavior and remaining resilient if changing conditions bring adversity.

Finally, adaptability requires dispositional flexibility, which is being receptive to change, having a "can do" attitude, being willing to alter working styles or approaches, and having the confidence to improvise, experiment, or switch courses quickly.

Chapter 8 ("Leading Change") will cover a special brand of adaptability: how leaders in the middle can effectively lead change. What follows are the most potent ways to quickly build your intellectual, emotional, and dispositional flexibility skills.

Skill Build #1: Practice the 50/50 Rule

When faced with conditions that require adaptability, focus 50 percent of your mental energy and actions on pragmatism and the other 50 percent on possibility. The pragmatism forces realism and a focus on problem solving (and thus granular progress) while possibility keeps you in the right frame of mind, viewing the emerging situation as an opportunity. And 50 plus 50 of course adds up to 100, which means 0 percent of your mental space can be given to negativity or a lack of self-confidence that would cause you to struggle to adapt. View your circumstances as happening *for* you, not *to* you. The only victim should be your victim mentality, which is of no use to the adaptable leader in the middle.

I have plenty to work on as a leader but I can say a strength is being able to turn on a dime and pivot when required. I credit use of the 50/50 Rule for this, along with my willingness to quickly break from the past when needed. I don't get hung up in how things were or the pain of shifting—I just shift to pragmatism and possibility. I've also learned when you expect much of yourself in times requiring adaptiveness and are self-confident along the way (recalling that you've navigated change successfully many times over), you build resilience, which makes the need to adapt in the future easier.

Skill Build #2: Use the OAR tool to vanquish your discomfort with uncertainty

OAR is an acronym I developed with the help of Mark Power, a Buddhist chaplain and fellow faculty member at Indiana University's Kelley School of Business for Executive Education (he's an expert at handling the discomfort and need to adapt that uncertainty triggers). In the face of uncertainty, simply Observe the uncertainty, don't Overreact to it. Acknowledge its presence, don't Attempt to control it by filling the unknown with misinformation and assumptions. Recognize that impermanence is inevitable (solidity is an illusion, fluidity is real) and Revel in the benefits uncertainty spurs like creativity, resilience, and agility. Practice this powerful acronym yourself and share it with your employees.

Skill Build #3: Practice finding the better third way

This is about embracing the spirit of crafting multiple solutions. Often when we create solutions, we stop at two, then pick which of the two is more palatable, which often isn't easy because both options come with tremendous tradeoffs. That's when you push forward to find the better third option, which has less tradeoffs all around. This is an adaptability skill that Procter & Gamble CEO David Taylor considers to be one of his central keys to success.

Skill Build #4: Embrace a spirit of experimentation

Experiments are like practice runs in adapting. You learn along the way, adjust, and move forward. The more experiments you encourage in your shop the more you feed a culture of experimentation and the more adaptable your organization becomes. For example, personally role model experimentation by trying something new or putting yourself in unfamiliar situations. Then, discuss the experience with your team and what you learned from it. It all adds up to adaptability.

Skill Build #5: Bolster your predictive capabilities

Being prepared, informed, and able to predict makes it easier to adjust on the fly. So be in tune with industry trends. Spend time scenario planning for the biggest problems your business could face. Do so with a diverse group of experts and include modeling for what you think competitors might or might not do in the face of the expected challenge (and in response to your response). Plot out specific courses of action for each scenario and get preapproval to resulting actions so that you can move fast when the time comes.

As an example, many times at Procter & Gamble I was part of scenario planning that we'd do before taking a price increase or launching a new product. We'd assemble a team to think through a variety of competitive response scenarios. Doing so improved our adaptability as we were more prepared for however the competitor ended up responding.

Skill Build #6: Stick to an intentional learning plan

Being exposed to learning opportunities is essential to building adapt-ability, as it gives you practice pressing forward into the unknown, absorbing new stimulus, and broadening your knowledge base to better inform future actions—all things that adapting requires. So fostering a learning environment is critical and deserving of your effort to create a specific learning plan. Start with this rule of thumb: 70 percent of learning should come from daily involvement in the job itself, 20 percent learning from others (including from coaching), and 10 percent from formal training (attending industry conferences or training sessions, for example).

We'll cover coaching in depth in Chapter 5 ("Leading Those Who Report to You"), but know that learning prompts are a powerful tool to use in your learning plan. A study from the University of Southern California illustrates what I mean. Researchers tracked results when leaders used a learning prompt with newly promoted executives every two weeks. The prompt was, "What have you done since we last talked, and what, if anything, have you learned from it?" The executives quickly started paying rapt attention to their growth because they knew the boss would be asking and were amazed at how much they were learning.[1] You can use this same tactic to show that you expect learning and growth. And when you couple it with having patience and empathy for the learning process (and tolerance for mistakes), adaptability blossoms.

Meshing

This is the ability to foster a collaborative spirit, to reconcile conflicting and changing priorities and viewpoints and get opposing forces with different agendas to come together as one. The middle manager with-out the meshing skill faces the inability to get anything accomplished. The obvious meshing moves are to build a foundation of trust within the organization, to encourage innovation (which forces trial runs in collaboration), and to have the right technology tools in place to enable collaboration. Less obvious (and just as powerful) are the methods that follow for building this critical skill.

Skill Build #1: Provoke the big picture

People unite when they have something bigger picture to unite for and rally behind. It can be a gripping cause or a powerful purpose, mission, or vision. It can be as simple as clear, compelling, and common goals. Whatever you rally people around, it should feel like it's something worth fighting for, something with a personal and emotional connection, something that, if accomplished, would have meaning to the "doers." In other words, not just a numerical target.

You further grow your meshing skills when you consistently keep the bigger picture in front of your group. You can do that by starting every townhall or team meeting with a reminder of what the collective group is fighting for. Use the big picture as a filter by asking (before actions are taken), "Will that help us move closer toward what we're ultimately trying to accomplish together?" Employees can easily forget the higher order objective when they're engaged in day-to-day struggles. Never underestimate how often you should amplify the bigger picture to remind employees of the reason they need to work together.

As an example, a consumer goods company I keynoted for conducts monthly "Collaboration Communications" (as they call them), monthly companywide meetings where leaders share the big picture of what the company is trying to accomplish and why collaboration is so important (in their case it fuels innovation). They also give awards out at these sessions to employees exhibiting great collaboration, which brings us to the next skill build.

Skill Build #2: Follow the 100:1 Ratio

This means for every one grand gesture you make that demonstrates how important collaboration is, you make 100 smaller, celebratory gestures. On the grand gesture front, you might not be able to do like Apple did and build a new HQ for your company with a massive park-like open space in the middle to encourage casual run-ins and idea sharing. But you can do a smaller grand gesture, such as build a "Collaboration Corner" like another one of my clients did, complete with open meeting space, a coffee bar, and high-tech whiteboards. Or maybe your grand gesture is a day of offsite training on collaboration.

More importantly, even with bigger plays in mind, the real power comes in recognizing and rewarding collaborative behavior in smaller ways, more consistently, like my consumer goods client. You can amplify collaborative tendencies by celebrating such behavior, frequently, on the spot even, until it starts to trickle down and around and become a cultural norm.

Skill Build #3: Remember the three C's of collaboration

The three C's are Clarity of roles, Community, and Conflict. First, to enable collaboration it's critical to clearly define everyone's role so each person knows their part on "the assembly line" and what the role is of others on the assembly line as well. This includes becoming familiar with each person's strengths across your team and leveraging them to best achieve collective goals.

It's also important to think community over corporation, meaning, look for opportunities to bring warmth and a sense of connectedness to your workplace to make it feel less like a cold entity. For instance, encourage open knowledge sharing, proudly celebrate successes and failures, and create opportunities to have fun and learn together. All of this helps build a shared team identity, which is like collaboration rocket fuel.

Finally, collaboration should not be confused with consensus. Research shows the ability to engage in healthy conflict is a leading indicator that a team will successfully collaborate and achieve their goals. So it's vital to move your group from being polite and guarded in communications with each other to being challenging (yet respectful), honest, and unafraid of productive conflict or healthy debate. There are many ways to do so. For example, you encourage healthy debate when you ensure everyone in a debate feels heard and keeps an open mind, when you ask for data to back up opinions, when you ask others to commend versus condemn the opposing point of view, when you ask that criticism be accompanied by a new idea or suggestion to improve the original idea, when you ensure debate remains focused on the point at hand and doesn't derail into personal attacks based on poor underlying relationships, and when you cut off "meeting hijackers" who constantly interrupt or drone on and cause others to disengage from the debate at hand.

Political Savviness

The presence of this as a vital skill to build may surprise you. After all, aren't others-oriented leaders in the middle anything but political, focused on others, not themselves? Yes, but there's a difference between being political and being politically savvy.

Leaders who are political engage in backstabbing, shameless self-promotion, maneuvering, rumor mongering, coercing, and untruths. They put their own interests before everyone else's and stand ready to gain personally at others' expense.

Leaders who are politically savvy advance their own interests, but most often in conjunction with the greater good and never at the expense of it or others. Political savviness means understanding, not manipulating. It's understanding the underlying context, issues, and personalities involved. It's another tool for the others-oriented leader to leverage to serve their organization and get things done without turning a blind eye to worthy personal benefit.

While you should avoid political behavior when leading from the middle, it's unwise not to sharpen your political savviness. After all, by being in the middle you're inevitably going to discover, in all directions, pockets of egos, rivalries, pet projects, turf wars, hidden agendas, sacred cows, and opposing factions. You're going to encounter people with differing levels of power, those who are extremely motivated by getting promoted and moving up (to a fault), those so passionate about their agenda that they're willing to bend the rules to achieve it, and those hell bent on winning the internal war for resources.

You can choose to ignore all of this or be savvy about operating within this reality to maximize your effectiveness. Figure 3.1 provides a self-assessment: a 25-question quiz that defines political savviness through its questions, with the questions coded into four categories:

1. Self-Image (SI)
2. Organizational Awareness (OA)
3. Organizational Assets/Tensions (OAT)
4. Others-Orientation (OO)

The yes-or-no answers to these questions will help you self-assess on this skill, with every "no" pointing to an opportunity to build your political savviness.

Locking In

Everything you should amplify as a talented middle manager is not always blatant and in your face. Alertness to the more "hidden" elements of your environment that require special attention is essential. Specifically, there are four micro-topics for you to laser in and lock onto, areas you're best suited to spot and address given your role in the middle. They're the four *C*'s of Hyper-awareness: Constraints, Capacities, Capabilities, and Culture.

	Yes	No
1. I'm able to exhibit impulse control and keep myself blurting out whatever I think. (SI)	☐	☐
2. I understand how decisions really get made and how things really get done in my company. (OA)	☐	☐
3. I know who the gatekeepers are (those who provide access to what I need). (OA)	☐	☐
4. I know who the key influencers are (those who have great influence on what I need). (OA)	☐	☐
5. I know who the key decision makers are. (OA)	☐	☐
6. I know who the key stakeholders are (those who care most about a decision). (OA)	☐	☐
7. I seek out genuine, value-added reasons for connecting with people who impact my career. (SI)	☐	☐
8. I understand the cultural and behavioral norms in my company. (OA)	☐	☐
9. I know what behaviors are highly encouraged in my company. (SI/OA)	☐	☐
10. I know what behaviors are considered unacceptable in my company. (SI/OA)	☐	☐
11. I have developed an effective partnership with my boss. (OAT)	☐	☐
12. I know who will resist my agenda and who I need on my side to advance it. (OAT)	☐	☐
13. When I score a victory, I make sure the other side can save face. (OO)	☐	☐
14. I have a sponsor (someone to provide support for my advancing in the organization). (OAT)	☐	☐
15. I engage in subtle, warranted self-promotion (versus over-the-top, gratuitous self-promotion). (SI)	☐	☐
16. I have good self awareness. (SI)	☐	☐
17. I have good situational awareness (I'm observant of what's happening in the moment). (OO)	☐	☐
18. I have good organizational awareness (I know what image my company wants to portray). (OA)	☐	☐
19. I'm intentional about making other people look good. (OO)	☐	☐
20. I don't change who I am on different occasions, just nuances of how I need to act. (SI)	☐	☐
21. I've built a network of friends and influencers across the company. (OAT)	☐	☐
22. I've built strategic alliances across the company. (OAT)	☐	☐
23. I'm open-minded and vocal about what I believe but mindful of how I express it. (SI)	☐	☐
24. I advocate strongly for my viewpoint, then commit to the final decision. (OO)	☐	☐
25. When in doubt, I let my values guide me to good decisions. (OO)	☐	☐

Key:
SI = Self-Image
OA = Organization Awareness
OAT = Organizational Assets/Tensions
OO = Others-Orientation

Your Score:
- You checked "Yes" 20–25 times: Politically astute - You're leveraging office politics in a highly effective and appropriate manner. Strengthen your strengths on this front.
- You checked "Yes" 9–19 times: Politically competent - You've got game, but there's plenty of low-hanging opportunity to be savvier and more effective. Turn each "No" into a "Yes."
- You checked "Yes" 0–8 times: Politically naive - You've got much to learn and practice to keep from getting steamrolled or self-sabotaging at work. Not to worry, political savviness is a skill that can be learned. Take it one step at a time; turn one "No" into a "Yes" then move on to the next one.

Figure 3.1 The Political Savviness Poll

Constraints

The Theory of Constraints states that the performance of any system is held back by constraints or bottlenecks that restrict output.[2] In other words, the chain is only as strong as its weakest link, its limiting factor. These constraints or limiting factors are the biggest things holding your business back. And the thing is, these constraints restrict output whether you acknowledge them or not. Too few mid-level managers put a concerted effort into identifying their hidden constraints, let alone addressing them as a fast route to significantly improved performance. Don't miss the opportunity. Working on just your biggest constraint will still have the biggest impact.

You can identify that constraint by conducting what's known as a "Why-Why-Why" analysis. I learned about this from product supply experts who work in huge manufacturing plants. They use this analysis to help determine bottlenecks that might be slowing down production on the line, but it's a tool with far broader use. Start with a problem that's holding you back from achieving your goals. As a simple example, let's say you're facing poor online sales. This problem, like many, may be glaringly obvious, but the constraint driving the problem most often is not. So, you dig, one layer at a time, by continually asking, "Why?" Why are you achieving poor online sales? You discover it's because you're not getting enough traffic to your website. Okay, why? Well, it's because your online advertising isn't generating enough clicks. Okay, why? Well, that's because you don't understand your target audience well enough to get them interested with a message worth clicking on. *Bingo*. Now you know what to do. You get the idea. You keep asking "Why?" until you've uncovered the true constraint or a clear path of action that solves the problem.

Capacities

The mid-level manager is in the best position to spot when the surrounding organization is reaching maximum capacity and starting to experience burnout. In 2019, the World Health Organization named burnout, which results from chronic workplace stress, an official medical condition and occupational hazard.[3] Burnout doesn't just

1. Employee always seems tired or has low energy
2. Disengagement and apathy
3. Increased cynicism and complaining
4. Decreased productivity and quality of work
5. Self-isolation (detaching from social aspects of work)
6. Irritability and over-sensitivity
7. Absenteeism and tardiness

Figure 3.2 The Seven Signs of Employee Burnout

happen overnight, it creeps up on employees over time, making it more difficult to spot. So, leaders in the middle have to be locked in enough to see the signals because employees often don't volunteer that information. To get eagle-eyed on this front, see Figure 3.2 for the seven most telltale signs of employee burnout, then we'll discuss what to do about them.

Whenever these signs start appearing often enough to indicate a trend, I've found it's very helpful to sit down with employees and, with great empathy, dig deeper. We'd discuss four hypotheses for their malaise (all rooted in the most common underlying causes of the chronic stress that leads to burnout):

1. Is it too much work? If this is the case, discuss priorities, how you can take nonessential work off your employees' plates, and any training they might need to be more efficient in their work.

2. Is it the wrong work? This leads to a discussion on whether or not the role is the right fit for the employee or a discussion on role clarity—ensuring the employee understands the expectations of their role, what's required and what isn't (acknowledging that they may have taken on things outside their scope of responsibility).

3. Are you getting the wrong response to your work? This uncovers if employees feel underappreciated for their efforts, or if they're running into unreasonable restraints, barriers, or toxicity in trying to get their work done. You can help here by dialing up the appreciation and helping them bust barriers.

4. Do you have unrealistic expectations of your work? I ran into this one a lot with high achievers. They had taken on an "I can, and must, do everything" mentality. This led to good discussions on setting realistic expectations and boundaries. If perfectionism was an issue, it led to good discussions on how to stop. For example, you can help employees see the corrosive impact their perfectionism is having on the total project, help them get past a fear of rejection or criticism, help them get good at "good enough," and help them to stop overestimating the negative impact of imperfection.

Capabilities

The most in-touch mid-level managers become very skilled at spotting three pivotal types of employees in particular, and acting accordingly when they do.

1. Rising stars. The need for skills in developing talent dramatically escalates at the mid-company level, which includes being able to spot individuals that can and should be moved up through the organization faster. I combined my personal experience in working at a leadership development hotbed for 24 years (Procter & Gamble) along with an intensive study of what key executives in a multitude of companies, big and small, felt were the key signs of rising star leaders. Clear themes emerged. Think of the paragraph that follows as a sort of mental checklist to aid you in spotting the stars (and helping them shine).

The best and brightest future leaders are able to learn quickly and adapt in the face of adversity. Learning and improving is of great importance to them, especially if it helps them achieve their goals. Rising stars are able to influence others through their personal power (not position power) and in general have a powerful personal presence (including communicating well and with confidence). They have an others-oriented approach, including having empathy, being a great listener, and having a service mindset but knowing when to step up and be more authoritative. Finally, they make consistently solid decisions based on data, experience, and judgment.

2. Everyday heroes. Every organization has them; the quieter, seasoned, often lower-level employees who work their tails off (often staying long after the leaders have gone home) and who know the systems and processes better than anyone. They're super-conscientious, über-efficient productivity machines, getting done whatever is asked and however much, with excellence and without complaint. And they typically do so without much recognition.

I learned over the years that these highly accountable, dependable bedrocks often don't want fancy recognition and heaps of rewards. They just want to be noticed, visibly valued, and to be given the respect they deserve. Make it a point to identify these everyday heroes in your organization, ask them questions to learn from their expertise, and go out of your way to let them know just how valued and valuable they are.

3. Unaddressed underperformers. Few things irk a star performer, or any employee, more than a corrosive, barely productive employee who continues their undesirable ways unchecked and unaddressed by management. It creates a sense of unfairness and the sentiment that either the leaders don't care enough to fix the problem employee or aren't in-tune enough with their organization to see the impact the underperforming employee is having. It's critical that you courageously address these chronic underperformers. Spotting them isn't as difficult as figuring out why they're underperforming. To help, here are the top reasons why employees don't do what they're supposed to:

- They think they're already doing it.
- They don't know why they should do it.
- They don't know what they're supposed to do.
- They don't know how to do it.
- They don't know when to do it.
- They think something else is more important.
- There's no positive outcome for their doing it.
- They're rewarded for not doing it.
- They're "turned off" by the type of work.
- There are circumstances beyond their control.

Use this list to help pinpoint the *why* behind the woeful performance, and then intervene accordingly.

Culture

You live and breathe the culture every day, but some diabolical, culture eroding elements require hyper-self-awareness to catch. And they have to do with you, directly. I'm talking about common, toxic little behaviors exhibited by well-meaning middle managers. There are seven in particular, the most common and caustic contributions you unknowingly make to your workplace culture. Avoid them all.

1. You're not resourcing the racehorses. By this I mean you're not paying enough attention to how you allocate resources. Specifically, you're not fighting to secure proper resources for your biggest priorities, your biggest bets (your racehorses). Instead, you might be making "more with less" the default mantra for everything. While that's a good efficiency war cry to adhere to in general, sometimes employees need to do more with more. Employees who consistently feel they aren't set up to win, especially without the resources they need on big priorities, will eventually become so frustrated they'll actually do less with what they currently have.

2. You're promoting only those who are like you. Step back and look at those you've promoted. Is there a common style to the promotees, absent of diversity? Are they people a lot like you? It's understandable, if so, as we're subconsciously drawn to those who are most like us. Be intentional and clear about what the criteria *really are* for getting promoted (ensuring that employees know, too) and ask yourself if you're adhering to them without bias.

3. You're unevenly giving recognition. This is about ensuring you're not just feeding the tallest sunflowers but are nurturing the entire garden. This is easily solved by starting from a place of caring about the entire organization and showing it, often, in big ways and small. I'm not talking about feeding the "everyone gets a trophy" mentality; recognition should always be warranted. I'm simply pointing out that giving recognition unevenly is just as toxic as not giving it at all.

4. You're passively enabling. As discussed in the Capabilities section above, you may be letting underperformers continue as such by not intervening. It's poisonous to a culture.

5. You underestimate the importance of information flow. You might think, "I don't want to flood them with too much" or "They don't really need to know this, they just need to stay focused on what they're doing." Reasonable thoughts. Slippery slopes. The key with any information you hold is to ask yourself, "Would this materially help the employees do their job better or understand something important?" And while it can take a lot of work to properly share information, it's worth it to avoid the cultural negatives. You don't want employees feeling out of the loop, unable to do their best work, undervalued, or untrusted.

6. You're not balancing reality with hope. There are two traps here. The first is bravely sharing a realistic, even if tough, picture of the current state of the business, but then failing to give employees hope that there's a way forward. The other trap is just as bad: painting a rosy, motivating picture of the future without having any of the aspirations grounded in reality. It's important to mindfully get the balance right.

7. You're role modeling the opposite of work–life balance. We'll discuss shortly the importance of setting the tone for your workplace, but few things you do have as direct a cultural and whole-life impact on your employees as whether or not you role model a positive balance, or integration, between work and life. Do so by firmly prioritizing and setting boundaries as we discussed in Chapters 1 and 2, by asking yourself before taking on any new work, "Is the juice worth the squeeze?" and by involving others in your quest for balance (like asking others not to keep you past meeting times, etc.).

Influence

When it comes right down to it, leadership is influence. Research from Cornell and Stanford Universities shows that we dramatically underestimate our ability to influence up, down, and across an organization.[4] And yet, no one has the potential to be more influential, and thus effective, than someone who leads from the middle. In fact, this entire book is intended to help you influence up, down, and across.

Standard influencing advice would say that to maximize your influence focus on things you can control (like what you say, how you behave, decisions you make), exude warmth (warmth being the gateway to influence as it fosters trust and a desire to connect), use the "yes" ladder (get people to agree to something small before gaining agreement to something bigger), spell out the cost of not doing something, leverage social proof (others are doing it), and use reciprocity (give something to others first so they feel compelled to give back, which we'll talk more about in Chapter 7, "Influencing Peers"). All good counsel.

But we're going to go beyond the beaten path to build your influencing ninja-skills, honing the most potent aspects of influencing that require targeted and specialized know-how. Specifically, we'll focus on building your skills in persuasive communication, influencing in meetings, and spotting and breaking patterns.

Ninja Skill Build #1: Persuade by being clear and concise

Make clear and concise your mantra by using the acronym SHARP (especially powerful for those who tend to ramble a bit):

- **S**tart by thinking, not talking. Doing both while explaining away your confusing oratory with the declaration "I think out loud" won't cut it. Pause to gather your thoughts before speaking, if it helps.

- **H**it the main idea quickly. Avoid filler words like "*umm*" and "like." Don't wander or your audience will wonder what your point is.

- **A**dd details sparingly. Don't overexplain. Provide just as much context as necessary.

- **R**elate to the audience. Know your audience and meet them where they're at. Know what they want (in fact put their needs first), why you're addressing them, what's in it for them, and tailor your approach accordingly. Be honest and vulnerable. Say "we" not "you." Be passionate about your topic and explain why you are.

- **P**repare. Winging it is the mortal enemy of being clear and persuasive.

Ninja Skill Build #2: Excel at nonverbal communication

Be a nonverbal ninja by using the acronym FESTER, intended as a reminder to keep nonverbal cues top of mind and to not let poor nonverbal skills fester.

- **F**acial expressions—watch for them as they're a treasure trove of information you can use to adjust your communications on the fly.

- **E**ye contact should be maintained, it's an easy way to connect.

- **S**pace must be given (if in a culture where close-talking is a turn-off).

- **T**one of voice is a powerful cue to inform how to proceed in your communications.

- **E**xpressive hand motions and gestures tell a lot, so watch for them.

- **R**ead posture as it conveys much about attitude, confidence, and state of mind.

Ninja Skill Build #3: Use persuasion tricks professional speakers use

Being a keynote speaker, I can share a half-dozen tricks of the trade in terms of persuasive communication, many of which CEO and politician speechwriter Simon Lancaster also subscribes to.[5]

1. Use juxtaposing soundbites. In one of my keynotes I use a line to grab leaders' attention about the power their words and actions hold in terms of building or busting others' self-confidence. Of this I say, "You can plant seeds of growth, or seeds of doubt." People tell me they remember that line. The juxtaposition presents tension and a sense of balance, which our brain likes and recalls.

2. Use stories. Paul Smith, business storytelling expert and author of *The 10 Stories Great Leaders Tell*, explained to me that compared to data and logic alone, stories make your communication more effective in almost every way that matters. Research suggests that compelling stories activate the subconscious, emotional-processing part of the brain where it turns out most of our decisions are actually made. As a result, your ideas will be more memorable, more apt to be spread by word of mouth, more inspiring, and more capable of influencing people's decisions and behavior than they would be without stories. What that means is that telling great stories will better equip you to influence what people think, feel, and do—in other words, leadership.

3. Use rapid-fire sentences to convey urgency. By this I mean speak energetically in a short, quick series of clipped, well-articulated sentences at specific points where you really want to communicate urgency. I use this technique when I really want to hammer home a point or drive an audience to action. Doing so requires having well-rehearsed those few sentences so they flow seamlessly, but the effort is worth it. It has the added benefit of giving the impression you're the subject matter expert. And when coupled with the use of well-placed seconds of silence, it's extra powerful. As an example, at one point in one of my keynotes, I really want the audience to feel the importance and urgency of the need to embrace change. So I say, in rapid-fire fashion, "If you choose to see change as a pivotal moment, a jumping-off point to step back and think bigger, a chance to change your trajectory professionally and personally, you'll do just that. You see because you can't get to what you yearn to be (long pause) *by remaining what you are* (long pause), change is the vessel." The combination of speed and silence underscores that I just said something important, which sticks with the audience.

4. Talk in threes.   We're used to things in threes. Three supporting points for a recommendation, three selling points to convince us, death seems to come in threes (notice I just used three points to make my argument). It just has a sing-song quality to it that's more persuasive.

5. Use metaphors (but sparingly).   Too many is too much, but a well-placed, simple metaphor can be powerfully persuasive and help you clearly communicate your idea in a way 1,000 words can't do. For example, in one of my keynotes, to demonstrate the importance of a leader liberally granting autonomy to employees, I compare it to the process by which power flows through a light bulb. When you flow enough power to a light bulb, it lights up, as do employees when you flow enough autonomy to them. But when you flow only a little power to the bulb, it flickers at best, never reaching its full illuminative capacity. The same is true when you flow only a little autonomy to a high-wattage employee—they'll never reach their full illuminative capacity, either. People remember metaphors, which means they'll remember you and what you're trying to convince them of.

6. Use exaggeration that's clearly exaggeration.   Over-the-top sentences echo how we speak in everyday life, which makes them well accepted. I use exaggeration in my keynotes for humor or to dial up passion behind a point that warrants extra persuasion. Exaggeration as stretching the truth is never, ever a good idea. Audiences can smell exaggeration a mile away. If it's not obvious exaggeration, don't do it.

Ninja Skill Build #4: Up your influence in email

We've all been there, when we hit send and five seconds later wish we hadn't. Here are five questions to ask yourself before hitting send if you want to ensure your email is a well-written, persuasive one. Try keeping them on a sticky note next to your computer screen as a reminder.

1. Will my reader instantly understand my goal in writing this email and why they're receiving it? State the reason for the email, right up front. If you can tie in the benefit to the reader for reading it, even better. Even better still if you can accomplish all of this in the headline.

2. Have I made it easy for the reader to be interested in what I have to say? You can grab their attention by describing a problem they care about or promising a benefit that matters to them.

3. Have I put the core content of the email into digestible chunks? This is a trick I learned in writing for Inc.com. Write the email as if it were going to be skimmed, which it probably will be.

4. Did I close the email being clear about the action requested and having made compliance desirable and easy? Ensure there's nothing left to block the reader from taking the action you want.

5. Is there redundancy or passive-aggressiveness in this email that can be removed? These are the two biggest traps that destroy persuasiveness. Our speech patterns are repetitive in nature, and with email being the closest written proxy to how we speak (other than texts), it's easy to fall into a repetitive speech-like pattern in your email. Catch redundancy and comb it out.

1. *"As per my last email..."* This sounds like an accusation that the last email was ignored. Instead use "If you don't mind my reinforcing a point I made before, only because it's so important."

2. *"Just a friendly reminder..."* We both know you're not trying to be friendly. Instead try "I honestly hate when people bug me about something, but I'm forced to be 'that guy/girl' here in reminding you that... because..."

3. *"Please let me know if I've misunderstood."* What you're really saying here is "We both know you've got this wrong." This one is the most disingenuous of all because the recipient knows you don't think you have it wrong at all. Instead, write: "I honestly could have this wrong, but..."

4. *"Any updates on this?"* If I were to open an email from you with this in it, I couldn't help but picture you peering over the top of my cubicle with arms crossed, feet tapping, and a resting jerk face. Try this test: Say "Any updates on this?" out loud to yourself without sounding snippy. Impossible. Here's an alternative: "I'm guessing you're swamped--so, sorry to bug you, but what's the latest on... It would help to know because..." Being brief in email is key so I'm not preaching verbosity in any of these alternatives, but this one requires a bit more couching.

5. *"According to my records..."* This sounds formal and uptight. Is this a cross-examination or an email? Some alternatives: "I honestly could have this wrong, but from what I think I know..." or, "The way I see it is..."

6. *"Going forward I'd prefer..."* "Going forward" presumptively says "You were wrong" and "I'd prefer" sounds passively dictatorial. Since you're requesting a different action based on displeasure with the way something was done in the past, it's best to pick up the phone on this one.

Figure 3.3 The Top Six Passive-Aggressive Email Phrases

It's also important to avoid the tendency to be passive-aggressive when trying to speed up the persuasion process. Figure 3.3 presents what research shows are the top six passive-aggressive email phrases used that cause people to shut down versus opening up to be persuaded.[6] I also suggest alternative phrases.

Ninja Skill Build #5: Use the Law of Opposites to influence in meetings

You become more effective in meetings by following the Law of Opposites. There's a reason why so many view meetings as wasteful, why so many are, and why so many of us dread them. Bad habits abound. But meetings are also a great opportunity to increase your influence. If it's your meeting, of course you can run better meetings (a topic for another day). If you're attending another's meeting, this is where you apply the law. Here's how it works; it's simple, but incredibly effective. Start by recognizing the most common dysfunctional behaviors that occur in the meetings, then do the opposite. Acting in the opposite way will actually stand out and draw others to you as the undesirable behaviors are so common.

For example, be the person who is always present when others are multitasking. Listen when others are talking. Provide helpful perspective when others are chiming in just to say something. Be heard when others aren't listening. Share ideas, ask insightful questions, or respectfully push back when everyone else is silent. Be data based when everyone else is emotional. Bring humanity and light heartedness to a cold meeting. Sound confident when others sound uncertain. When others are confused or are adding to the confusion, help clarify and reframe. When others avoid accountability, raise your hand and own it. Be supportive when others are attacking. Be prepared when others aren't. Know the audience when others don't. When a meeting is spiraling out of control, bring it back on track.

For any bad meeting habit that you see, and there are plenty, commit to do the opposite. If it helps, in the margins of your meeting agenda, write down "do the opposite" as a reminder for you to do just that when you see unhelpful behaviors arise.

Ninja Skill Build #6: Become pattern aware

Leading from the middle means you're in the best position to observe and uncover patterns that could influence strategies and actions (positively or negatively). Make it a thing to get good at spotting patterns by increasing your powers of observation. This happens, for example, when you conduct analysis with the desire to spot trends and spend more time staying close to consumers, customers, competitors, and your own organization.

Even more powerful is when you can break patterns that aren't serving the business well. For example, say you spot old tapes playing—old, tired narratives and excuses that have people in your organization stuck in an unproductive loop. You break this pattern by calling out assumptions when you hear them, by asking why it's believed those assumptions are true, and by challenging language like "never," "always," "all of," or "none of." Creating tension with an unhelpful status quo is tremendously influential because it changes mindsets and helps people get out of their own way. Now multiply this kind of impact by the number of bad patterns you spot and break and you get a sense for the importance of becoming pattern aware.

Fostering Compromise

In many of the interviews I conducted, one of the first skills that mid-level managers mentioned as being required to excel at their jobs was the ability to foster compromise. It makes sense given the variety of opposing interests up, down, and across an organization and how the middle manager, in the middle of it all, must broker the peace to move things forward. So how do you do so?

The Golden Rules of Compromise

What follows is help for building the skill of fostering compromise, assuming that you're serving as a coordinating party between two factions in need of compromise. These are the "golden rules":

1. Establish common bonds. In a negotiation study between MBA students at two business schools, some groups were told "Time is money. Get straight down to business." Fifty-five percent in this group struck an agreement. The other groups were told, "Before you begin negotiating, exchange some personal information with each other and identify a similarity you share in common." Ninety percent in this group came to an agreement (with outcomes worth on average 18 percent more to both parties).[7] The study showed the power of two sides establishing common bonds before trying to strike a compromise.

You can facilitate this between two parties by providing that bond—reminding all of the common objectives, goals, or common enemy (competitor). You can also mirror the study and ask both sides to engage in a personal sharing session before you discuss the topic requiring compromise.

2. Create "That's right" moments. This is a trick of former FBI hostage negotiator, Chris Voss.[8] It's about making sure both sides understand and articulate the other's wants, desires, goals, and fears. When one side articulates these things regarding the other, it triggers the "That's right" response. Defenses start going down with each affirmation, and compromise starts warming up.

3. Cut off catastrophizing. As discussion continues, don't allow either side to begin overstating what they'd really lose if they were to compromise. Ask them that opinions, of their own situation and that of the other, be grounded, not unfounded.

4. Help both sides understand the Law of Concessions. This states that in achieving effective compromise, both sides, by definition, must make concessions. Establish this law up front to ensure that both sides start from a place of good faith. The idea is to establish that a cooperative framework is in place versus a combative one. In so doing, you're asking all involved to keep an open mind.

5. Encourage animated, but not heated, debate. Compromise is hard work, sure to stir emotions. That's good, because you want truth and passion to come out so both sides get the full picture of the other's situation. Just keep the passionate discussion at an animated level (energetic and excited), intervening when it starts moving to heated (overly aggressive and tinged with anger).

You Set the Tone

No one sets the tone of an entire organization more than those who lead from the middle. And there are so many ways to set the tone on so many things, so let's keep this simple. Earlier in this chapter I covered the most common toxic things you can unwittingly do to set a negative tone. Here, I share the three most vital rules for setting a positive tone that will have the biggest positive ripple impact on the most people.

1. Remember the "Fishbowl Effect."   When you're in the middle you live in a fishbowl, with everyone watching from all sides. You get the behaviors you tolerate *and* exemplify. Never forget that what you say and how you act can stick in the minds of those around you for longer than you ever imagined.

2. Exude trust and transparency.   You set the most important tone of all, one of trust, by exhibiting unswerving transparency. Research shows there are six specific forms of transparency that are particularly powerful for building trust. That is, when you show transparency:

- in the information you share and how you share it
- in "state-of-the-union" updates you give about the business
- about why you made a decision
- by being honest with people about where they stand
- in being honest about your shortfalls
- in being open about your agenda (knowing that hidden agendas rarely remain as such)

3. Live the "Attitude Anthem."   I'm referring here to a quote I kept on my office door for years, reminding me of one of the most powerful, far-reaching, tone-setting behaviors I could put on display to positively influence the culture. It's from author Charles Swindoll: "Life is 10 percent what happens to you and 90 percent how you react to it."[9]

Having now covered the general skills needed to be a successful manager in the middle, think of the chapters that follow as the "specialty skills" required. Let's go run those plays.

Notes:

1. M.W. McCall Jr., "Recasting Leadership Development," *Industrial and Organizational Psychology* 3, no. 1 (February 16, 2010).

2. "Theory of Constraints (TOC)," Theory of Constraints Institute, tocinstitute.org (2019).

3. "QD-85 Burn-out," icd.who.int.

4. V. Bohns and F. Flynn, "Underestimating Our Influence Over Others at Work," digitalcommons.ilr.cornell.edu (2013).

5. S. Lancaster, "Tap Into the Power to Persuade by Using These 6 Techniques of Clear and Compelling Speech," idea.ted.com (September 9, 2019).

6. K. Guzdek, "The Business Jargon and Buzzwords You Love to Hate," getresponse.com (August 9, 2019).

7. "Principles of Persuasion," influenceatwork.com.

8. C. Voss, "5 Tactics to Win a Negotiation, According to an FBI Agent," *Time*, time.com (May 25, 2016).

9. brainyquote.com.

4 Leading Your Boss

A nyone who has ever had a boss knows that effectively influencing and interacting with said boss can be tricky and even angst inducing. Those who do it best realize that it's not just one of the many relationships you must manage while leading from the middle, it's the opportunity for a full-on partnership, one vital for business success and that's two times more critical for your career success than any other relationship, according to a McKinsey study.[1] Being held in high regard by your boss is one of the most powerful forms of influence and visibility you can wield. Not to mention that if you want to be considered good at managing people (which most of us do), people includes your boss.

In this chapter, you'll learn how to build a partnership with your boss (and even their boss), step by step, play by play, with a method proven over three decades of research and experience. Understand that in attempting to create a great partnership with their boss, too many try to do too much, too soon, or skip critical actions that dramatically compromise the quality of the collaboration further down the line. But you can step up to a power partnership by following The Managing Up Staircase (as shown in Figure 4.1). Let's take it one step at a time.

Step 1: Nature Before Nurture

First and foremost, before you can nurture anything, it's important to understand and embrace the fundamental nature of an effective boss

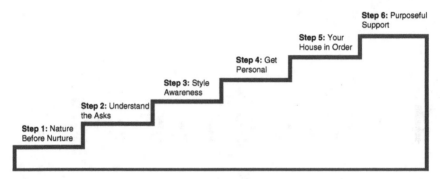

Figure 4.1 The Managing Up Staircase

and subordinate relationship. That is, *it's interdependence between two imperfect human beings.*

Full stop.

Many employees struggle with their boss because they gloss over this truth. You need your boss, and they need you. And you're both imperfect human beings.

Still, I've seen more frustrated employees than I can count reach the conclusion that they don't need their boss, that the boss is just an impediment to success. Or they hammer their boss for their mistakes and flaws, labeling them in an unrecoverable way. If you don't start by embracing the nature of the boss–subordinate relationship, the ideas of interdependence and fallibility, you can't begin to nurture anything. Not only will you never reach true partnership with your boss, your basic relationship is doomed to fail.

I'm not saying it's easy. The nature of the boss–subordinate relationship is filled with tension inherent in a hierarchy. For example, the boss plays fundamentally conflicting roles, as supporter and assessor. How much do you reveal of what you need when, at the same time, your boss is evaluating and judging your abilities? Managing this particular tension is about establishing a trusting relationship so the roles of supporting and evaluating are no longer at odds. In general, though, the first step in the Managing Up Staircase is about missteps, and avoiding them. What follows are the five most common mistakes to avoid as the subordinate in the boss–subordinate relationship.

1. Managing up is not sucking up

Your boss will see through apple-polishing behavior. Nor is it about being a "yes" person or mini-me replica of the boss. Don't lose yourself in trying to find a bond. Which brings us to the next common misstep.

2. Deference is not an obligation, nor is resistance always right

Effective leaders from the middle don't approach the nature of their relationship with their boss as being on either end of a spectrum. Meaning, on one hand, they aren't mindless "yes" people. They realize that always deferring to the boss and following the path of least resistance leads nowhere good. Nor are they at the other extreme, feeling it's their duty to be antagonistic to the boss at every turn. It's about striving for balance, knowing when to push back and when situational followership is called for. Getting the balance right is a basic, but critical, early step toward partnership.

Regarding being too deferential, this is where most of us struggle. The key here is to be honest with yourself about your tendency to be dependent on authority figures. If you tend to fall right into line or look too much to the boss for what to do, ask yourself if that tendency is really serving you, your boss, and your organization in the best way possible. The answer, of course, is no.

Regarding pushing back on your boss, later in this chapter we'll discuss how to disagree with them. For now, just remember that while yes, you should speak truth to power, every exchange doesn't have to be a power play. If your default is to push back, think of how draining it would be if a subordinate continually did that to you. Pick your places.

3. Managing up shouldn't come at the expense of managing down

I've seen it too many times. Mid-level managers who are absolute champs at managing up. They have the boss eating out of their hand. But they're not feeding their employees. In fact, they largely ignore or vastly underserve their employees, figuring the time and energy is best spent managing up, to produce the most direct benefit for them personally. Think of managing up as an extension of managing down; it's for the benefit of your organization, too (not just for personal gain).

4. Your boss doesn't have extrasensory perception

I've seen many a boss–subordinate relationship go sour because the employee assumed the boss should be able to discern far more than you could expect from any human being. Even the most emotionally intelligent bosses aren't mindreaders. If you don't share what you need, what's troubling you, what's frustrating you, odds are it won't be divined by your boss. Assume that in the absence of communicating all of this to your boss, you'll get mediocre help at best. Don't assume what they know or should be doing and certainly don't make assumptions about their intent. Ask or tell and ye shall receive, or at least they'll now perceive, and can go from there.

5. Your boss doesn't define you

Yes, the leader from the middle must be able to lead upwards. But when the relationship becomes too all-encompassing, when you start to feel defined by how you think your boss perceives you, trouble follows. You'll compromise far too many things in your efforts to win your boss's approval. You might do things you wouldn't normally do that don't make you feel good or that aren't necessarily helping the relationship. As mentioned in an earlier chapter, seeking such acceptance is an empty pursuit at best, soul-crushing at worst.

Chase authenticity, not approval.

Put a cap on how much of your self-worth you derive from your manager's perceptions of you. Doing so takes some of the natural tension out of the relationship because you're only letting it mean so much to you. Should you try to exhibit limitless patience with your boss? Absolutely. Should you feel limited by what your boss thinks of you? Absolutely not.

Step 2: Understand the Asks

I'm betting that everyone reading this understands the importance of knowing what your boss expects from you. *Duh.* The problem lies in the assumptions we make and the lack of thoroughness on this front. Bosses rarely spell out exactly what they expect from the subordinate, and the subordinate too often falls short of fully comprehending. I conducted research among 200 pairs of bosses and subordinates to understand just how well the bosses' expectations were understood by the subordinates. In over *80 percent* of the pairings there were material breaches.

To close the comprehension gap, ask the right questions of your boss, the ones that tease out the nuances of what they're really expecting (and that help them better articulate it). Those questions are the ones that follow; specifically, nine of them. Ask your boss these questions even if you think you have a good handle on what's expected of you. They've been proven over my career to be extremely clarifying and to drive full alignment on expectations between boss and subordinate.

1. "What does good performance look like? Great performance?"

Asking about the difference between good and great on anything (performance, leadership, risk taking, etc.) is extremely clarifying and helps you understand exactly what great looks like to your boss. What you thought was great may actually only be meeting base expectations in the eyes of your boss.

2. "Let's assume I'll get great results—what behaviors do you want/not want to see as I achieve those results?"

Bosses rarely spell out cultural expectations, i.e. *how* they want you to achieve the results that you do.

3. "What business metrics/goals are the most important to you and why?"

The "why" part is magic here. For example, you knew your boss cared about you hitting your profit target. But what if you learned that your boss missed his profit target a few times in the past and nearly lost his job because of it? You get the idea.

4. "These are my top priorities—are they consistent with yours?"

Bosses want to know that their overall agenda is being supported and that you're putting the right resources on the right things.

5. "This is how I'm spending my time—does it feel like it's supporting what's most important?"

This one is similar to the above, but is intended for bosses who are more detail oriented and for scenarios when business results are falling short. It's especially in these times that the boss can't help but wonder how the subordinate is spending their days and whether or not it's on the right things. Earn credit for at least putting your effort in the right places by asking this question.

6. "What measures does your boss most frequently discuss with you?"

Just like you care about what your boss focuses on with you, so should you care about what their boss focuses on. Knowing that further clarifies what's important to your boss, which you can then work to overdeliver on, which is basic to forging a great relationship.

7. "What specifically will get you promoted?"

This assumes your boss cares about getting promoted, of course.
It's a powerful question because it goes beyond the obvious answer,
"Great results will get me promoted." It helps flesh out the full picture
and nuances of what will make your boss look really good. That's
an itch you want to scratch and an opportunity to overdeliver on
expectations.

8. "What should I stop, start, and continue doing to better succeed?"

This gets to the thoroughness of understanding your boss's expectations and helps them articulate what may be bothering them about
your shortfalls (as well as help you identify what's working).

9. "Think of the most effective employee you've ever had working for you. What made them so effective?"

Bosses have unarticulated biases, like we all do. Even if you're delivering the goods, they may subconsciously be expecting you to deliver
results in the mold of a favored employee. It would help to know that.
This question is a good bridge into the next step in the Managing Up
Staircase.

Step 3: Style Awareness

I've seen so many potential boss–subordinate partnerships never come
close to fruition because the subordinate never took the time to understand the boss's style, and to then adapt to it. You might not like adjust-
ing your style to accommodate your boss's, but it's the lowest hanging
fruit there is for achieving an effective partnership.

The power of this step comes from acknowledging and acting on
the six key aspects of style that follow.

1. Information Receipt and Retention

Since a fair amount of the boss–subordinate relationship is about exchanging information, it's important to understand your boss's style preferences on this front and to accommodate. For example, do they prefer to communicate in email or in person? Do they process information better by listening or reading? Do they get impatient if you veer off topic or do they enjoy the sidebars? Finally, how much information on what kind of things do they want or not want? By the way, they tend to want more information than you think. And it's important to note that research shows the number-one piece of information bosses want is a progress report, that is, an update on progress on a project of interest.[2]

2. Decision-Making

Knowing how your boss likes to make decisions makes you more effective in influencing what they ultimately decide. Do they like to "stew and chew" or decide quickly? How much information, of what kind, do they need before they'll decide? Do they prefer consensus or just want to gather the information from different parties and make the final call? Do they prefer a firm recommendation from you or just the set of options? Do they prefer to be involved in all decisions or want to delegate as many of them as possible? Are you clear on your decision-making space? The more of this you know and act on accordingly, the more influential you'll be. Later in this chapter, you'll get help on how to proactively lead your boss's thinking in making decisions, thus further increasing your influence.

3. Conflict

Does your boss like conflict or tend to avoid it? Do they go guns blazing into an argument or prefer a subtler approach to influencing? Do they prefer disagreement behind closed doors versus out in the open? If you know your boss likes conflict, you can help them be ready for "battle" by arming them with convincing data and arguments. That's influence. If you know your boss doesn't like conflict, you can avoid putting them in uncomfortable situations and help them advance their agenda in non-confrontational ways. That's also influence.

4. Formality

Does your boss like a lot of structure or to adhere to strict processes? Are they more formal in style or informal? Differences in styles here can create unintended impressions on performance. For example, if you continually show up for your one-on-one with your boss without a thoughtful, written agenda, they may start to see you as undisciplined, a poor thinker, or worse. On the other hand, if you're too stiff and formal when your boss would rather be more free flowing, the impressions aren't much better. This is the easiest style difference to spot, even if it requires more effort to adjust to.

5. Task versus People Orientation

This is one that mid-level leaders often miss. The first aspect of it relates to your boss's perceived demands on their time and whether or not they feel they have a lot of time for you. They may prefer to spend more of their time driving tasks, projects, and timelines rather than meeting with you (even though the latter is much of how the former gets done). The second aspect of this is that when your boss does make time for you, they might prefer to talk about tasks, timelines, and project details versus spending a lot of time talking about your people. This one is tricky for others-oriented leaders who want to make sure their people's strengths are properly highlighted up the chain. Doing so, of course, is still an absolute must for you, even if your boss isn't a "people person."

As with so much in the middle, it's about striving for a balance (one your boss can live with), that is, knowing when too much people focus is too much or knowing when it's time to "get down to business" with your boss. Spending exorbitant amounts of time (in your boss's eyes) discussing people matters can lead to unfair and unhelpful impressions about you being too "soft" or distracted from running the business effectively (as misguided as that may sound). On the other hand, being all business all the time can make you seem uncaring and lacking in emotional intelligence.

6. Behavioral

This is about knowing the behavioral traits that make your boss most comfortable (or uncomfortable) in the working relationship; what annoys them or creates bonds. Strong partnerships are more likely when both sides pay respect to the other's personality trait preferences. And it should start with you. This isn't about being a fake version of you, but simply paying attention to what works with your boss (or not) and making slight adjustments in your approach. To help this along, I asked my bosses to think of a past team member they dreaded or relished working with and to tell me why in each case. The "stop, start, continue" question from Step 2 will also help discern which of your behaviors are working or not working for your boss. As will the next step.

Step 4: Get Personal

This is the fourth step, versus one of the very first steps, for a reason. Getting your boss to truly open up about themself is more likely when the basic "rules of engagement" and a baseline of trust have been established (via the first three steps). If you can get away with getting personal earlier, great. It's ultimately more important that you just make the effort to do so because a personal relationship forms the strongest roots of an effective and rewarding boss–subordinate partnership.

So how to get personal without overstepping? Have an agenda for learning about them, and work it over time, slowly getting them to share more and doing the same in return to build rapport. Reward their confidence with absolute discretion.

But do have a plan. Here are some things to seek to understand about them:

- Understand their pressures, aspirations, hopes, and fears.
- Understand what matters most to them in their life.
- Ask what they like most about their workday and least about it.
- Find out what they worry about most and what makes them the most uncomfortable.
- Learn what motivates/energizes them, and what drains their energy.
- Find out what they feel are their superpowers (greatest strengths), weaknesses or blind spots, regrets, and biggest accomplishments.
- Discover their pet peeves and hot buttons.

The key is to make true connections versus trying to schmooze.

Step 5: Your House in Order

This is a gut-check step, critical to conduct right before the bulk of the work in managing up happens in Step 6. To manage up well, you have to be managing yourself well. That is, you must ensure you have your house, the basics of your job, in order. Otherwise your boss will be too distracted that you don't have a firm grip on your core job to engage in anything else. Here are the five gut-check, do I have my act together questions that discern if you're set up to manage up.

1. Are you delivering the results expected of you?

The foundation of a good boss–subordinate relationship is always about performance. If you're not getting results (or are getting them

while leaving bodies behind), the underlying relationship with your
boss will always be strained and efforts that don't tie directly to
improving results won't matter much. If you aren't getting the results
required, own it and show your boss you're doing what it takes to
change your outcomes. As an example, one of the best partnerships
I ever developed with a boss happened during a time when my business
results weren't great. I turned complete focus to turning the business
around, not worrying about the relationship with my boss, per se.
I was just sure to enroll him every step of the way on what we'd done
wrong and were doing to correct it, always with complete transparency.
The earnestness went a long way. Eventually, results, and the relationship with my boss, were terrific—and I credit the painful acceptance of
needing to "get my house in order."

2. Do you know your business, inside and out?

Your boss can't consistently fill knowledge gaps for you that shouldn't
be there without it eventually taking a toll on your relationship. Be
honest with yourself if your understanding of the fundamentals
of your business is spread too thin and is nowhere deep enough. Again,
take ownership. Invest in gaining expertise until you know enough to
lead those above you who want to know that you know enough. And
again, as mentioned in Chapter 1, it's not about being omnipotent,
it's about knowing enough of the right things and leveraging your
knowledge system to give your boss unswerving confidence that
"you've got things covered."

3. Have you asked for what you need?

You can't deliver if you don't put yourself in a position to deliver.

4. Are you organized and prepared for interactions with your boss?

Have a system in place that allows you time to prepare for one-on-ones
with your boss and have thoughtful agendas ready to go. If your boss

doesn't see you being intentional and in control of your time with him or her, they'll tend to assume you're not fully in control of your business.

5. Are you bringing the attitude you want reciprocated?

It's hard to expect your boss to have a good attitude toward you or to bring enthusiasm, dependability, or high integrity to the table (or anything else you crave in the relationship) if you don't put it on display first.

Step 6: Purposeful Support

This step is the "heavy lifting" on the Managing Up Staircase, where you put in the hard work to support your boss, to be a go-to player, to move the business forward, to make them look good, and to leapfrog your way to partnership. It's called purposeful support to distinguish itself from blind support, where you're just taking orders and doing whatever the boss says. The support you offer should be intentional about the *why* and *how* to make your spirit of servitude more meaningful. It's not about impressing your boss (although that's certainly a great side effect), it's about performing well in your duty to support your boss. To do so, know that there are six core areas your boss most values your support on and that most directly lead to a spirit of true partnership.

1. Information

Keeping your boss fully informed (or at least as informed as they want to be as mentioned previously) takes real work; it's an investment you can choose to make, or not. But think about it for a moment. How can you have a partnership with anyone, on anything, if you're not keeping them up to date in as thorough, accurate, and timely fashion as they require? One mid-level manager I spoke to told me he divides his weekly one-on-ones with his boss into two, 30-minute halves, labeled as such on his agenda: "What you need to know" and "What I need from you."

2. Capacity

Managing up effectively includes expanding your boss's capacity, which can be hard to swallow given how busy you already are while leading from the middle. But even the act of asking your boss, "What's overwhelming you now and how can I help?" goes a long way toward partnership. Your boss may or may not take you up on the offer, but at a minimum, they'll appreciate your others-orientation. And use a simple rule I used very effectively for decades: take more things off their plate than you put on it.

3. Decision-Making

We talked earlier in this chapter about understanding how your boss generally likes to make decisions. This is about actually leading your boss's thinking on this front. It starts with being emotionally intelligent. Of course, keep in mind your boss's decision-making style, but also consider how your boss wants to *feel* about your attempt to influence decisions, which certainly isn't as if they're being overly directed or manipulated. Bosses want to feel like you're enhancing their ability to make decisions, which you do by organizing, simplifying, and controlling the context in which they make them. To do that, use the following "context checklist" to simplify decision-making for your boss while helping you frame and influence those decisions.

- Present a clear set of choices with rationale and watch outs for each—choices make people more likely to choose and take action.
- Spend as much time defining the problem as providing solutions—a problem well-defined is one well-solved.

- Spend as much time prepping for questions as framing the answers—anticipating questions and answering them well provides instant added context and speeds decision-making.

- Provide perspective from sources they'd seek—it's not about forcefully arguing your recommendation in a vacuum but proactively providing multiple points-of-view your boss would seek anyway in making a decision.

- Make the case for your preferred choice, but be honest about the shortfalls—this shows your thoroughness and puts the boss in solution mode versus "seeking more info" mode.

4. Problem-Solving

Few things bring as much sheer value to your partnership as when you bring a problem-solving spirit to the table. For example, make it a point to spot problems your bosses didn't know they had. Enhance your ability to do so by inviting employees to highlight issues (without "shooting the messenger"). Be as specific as possible in defining the problem (the root cause, not the symptoms) and why it exists, while being careful not to rush to solutions until the issue is fully understood. When ready, present multiple possible solutions with carefully considered pros and cons, knowing that the best solutions often lie within the definition of the problem itself. Also, be mindful not to inadvertently present problems in the form of complaints without having a proposal for how to address that complaint. You might not always have the solutions (your boss is there to help, after all), but thinking for yourself and having a problem-solving spirit won't go unnoticed.

5. Advocate

You support your boss when you advocate for them, just as you hope they do for you. This isn't about bootlicking; it's about taking or making opportunities to genuinely praise your boss or have praise and appreciation funneled toward them by others. Get to know your boss's boss and find sincere ways to let your two-up know when your boss is hitting it out of the park. Do it quietly. The odds are your boss will find out you've been praising them, which can only add to the partnership vibe. And you'll have done so without risking being seen by others as a suck-up.

6. In Process

Partnerships with your boss blossom not only from what you provide support on, but how you provide it. In the process of supporting your boss, be mindful of these things in particular:

- Treat your boss's time as if it were your own. Selectively use their time (and resources) and be super-efficient when you do. It's one of the most basic forms of respect you can show.

- Admit mistakes quickly and avoid unwanted surprises. Bury neither of these, no matter how painful. It feeds trust.

- Ensure your opinion is heard but don't overstep your bounds or try to upstage your boss. It erodes trust.

- Be proactive and take initiative. Who doesn't love someone who does?

- Be a constant source of positive energy. Who doesn't love someone who is?

Specialty Steps

Four topics deserve special consideration as you make your way up the Managing Up Staircase.

1. Disagreeing with Your Boss

It can be unnerving to disagree with your superior, but you owe it to the business, your boss, your organization, and yourself to do just that when called for. Remember these key points to disagree in a partnership-preserving manner.

Use respectful candor. In fact, strike an agreement with your boss for mutual candor long before the first disagreement has a chance to surface. Clarify that when the time arises to disagree, it will always be done with respect. Then reinforce it when the disagreement comes by starting with something like, "I want to remind you that I respect you, your point of view, and your position, but I'm in a different place than you on this. May I disagree and explain why?" This opening salvo sets up your candor in a way that will be better received as it's cloaked in respect and acknowledgment of authority.

Discuss intent before content. Social scientist Joseph Grenny indicates that dissent is often viewed as a threat to your boss's goals. Grenny says when your boss acts defensive, it's "far less often provoked by actual content than perceived intent."[3] Think about yourself when you're at your most defensive; you're probably assuming bad intent from the other party. To defuse this problem, give context as to why you're disagreeing, framing it in a mutual goal that your boss also cares about.

For example, say something like, "We're both trying to achieve maximum market share here, but ... " This signals why you're disagreeing. If you don't couch it in terms of mutual goals, your boss may view your disagreement as a lack of commitment to their interests.

Avoid judgment words. Stay humble and be careful about the language you use, avoiding accusing phrases like "You should have," "You shouldn't," or "You can't," replacing them with "I"-centered statements like "The way I see it is," or "I think differently on this one because ... " Your disagreement should feel like it's your perception, not personal.

2. Dealing with Bad Bosses

There are so many types of bad bosses that I can't possibly cover all the iterations here. Instead, I want to focus on the proven key plays to run to maximize your chance of at least salvaging a relationship with a terrible boss, regardless of the type.

Don't label. When you mentally or verbally label your boss as hopelessly arrogant, incompetent, uncaring, etc., you've put up another big barrier between you and any hope of a good relationship, let alone partnership. To prevent labeling, keep the next point in mind.

Know that you're only seeing part of the picture. No boss or employee wakes up wanting to be terrible. The odds are quite high that something is going on behind the scenes contributing to their overall odiousness. As painful as it might be, return to Step 4 in the Managing Up Staircase to get personal. Try to discern what else might be going on in your boss's life if they'll share. Bring empathy, not animosity, to the table.

Be mindful of their moods and triggers. Why set them off unnecessarily? Talk to others that have at least weathered working for your boss to learn more here, and to learn more in general about how to operate with him or her.

Be respectful of the position, if not the person. If things don't start to improve, remember it's important to hold at least the position your boss holds in high regard. Hierarchy has been around forever for a reason.

Turn your boss's weaknesses into opportunities for you to shine.
I'm not saying to upstage your boss, just to draw strength from the fact that you have the opportunity to better serve your organization by helping offset your boss's shortcomings. That's a far better path forward than letting your anger toward your boss escalate.

Assume you'll have to do 80 percent of the work.   Having a bad boss means you'll likely have to work much harder at the relationship than they're willing to and be far more flexible to adapt to their challenging traits. Nobody said it was fair. It most certainly isn't. But it's something you must learn to accept.

But also know when to draw the line. Be firm and confident in how you deal with your bad boss and clear on what behavior you simply can't tolerate.

Want to change the relationship as much as you need to.   You have to genuinely want to fix the relationship and put in the effort to do so (again remembering that the burden will likely fall disproportionately on you). Merely complaining won't change anything. The easy thing is to avoid the problems you're having with your boss. The right thing is to address those problems. The most efficient and effective way to do that is to give the horrific boss feedback, which we cover next.

3. Giving Your Boss Feedback

Whether you have a bad boss or just one who could benefit from some feedback (which is all of them), the thought of giving that feedback can be daunting. But it doesn't have to be. We'll cover the art and science of giving feedback to your employees in the next chapter. Sharing feedback with your boss deserves its own consideration. So, follow the points given here (they're applicable to any kind of boss).

Confirm your boss is open to feedback.   To find out, ask. Here's an effective way in: "I have some observations to share about you that I think could help you improve and/or achieve your goals. Is it okay if I share them?" Many times, I was surprised at the response. Bosses I thought would not be open to feedback were quite receptive—those who need it most aren't always blind to the fact. If they aren't open to receiving feedback, it's going to be very difficult to achieve a true partnership. You may have to adopt a "this too shall pass" approach in that case and wait it out until your boss moves on, or until you decide to do so.

Proceed with bravery. This is especially important if you have a bad boss. It's important that your boss comprehends the full impact that their opportunity areas are having on you, your co-workers, and the business. Watering down what you have to say or avoiding it altogether helps no one. That said, frame your feedback as your perceptions versus being accusatory in tone, saying things like "I noticed in that meeting you came across as harsh and unwilling to listen." Share observations, not presumptions, knowing that a common error is seeming too presumptive, like you don't realize that you only have a partial picture of what your boss deals with.

Be direct, honest, and specific as well as respectful and empathetic. Most bosses don't realize the full extent of the negative impact their actions or behaviors are having. The truth, even carefully presented, may sting, but in the long run the vast majority of bosses will appreciate you being brave enough to share the feedback.

Know that feedback is not the time for comparisons. Your boss won't like you comparing his/her performance to another great boss you've had, or worse yet, comparing to what you would do if you were boss. I doubt you'd like that, either. The only comparison that matters for your boss is to who they were yesterday and whether or not they're improving. With your feedback, you can help them get there.

Managing Multiple Bosses

This scenario can be quite common for those who lead from the middle. The key here is not to get caught between two sets of unrealistic expectations. The most important thing you can do is to get boss A to talk to boss B. Anyone who has ever had multiple bosses knows how challenging it can be, including your bosses, so they'll likely be receptive to it. If you don't get them talking about conflicting messages they're giving you or unrealistic demands they're collectively placing on you, each one will continue to operate in a vacuum, assuming they are your top priority and thus setting you up to burn out, fail, or both. So be firm in setting boundaries, and whatever work must be sacrificed to accommodate, assure the "victimized" boss that it's in the name of helping you to do a higher quality job on the true priorities.

To illustrate, one mid-level manager I interviewed worked in a matrixed organization where having two bosses was the norm. She had a quarterly meeting with her two bosses where she covered the same three topics each time: her collective priorities, conflicting messages/requests, and boundaries.

Now that you're well-equipped to forge a strong partnership upward with your boss, it's time to shift your attention down the organization to those who work for you.

Notes:

1. T. Barta and P. Barwise, "Why Effective Leaders Must Manage Up, Down, and Sideways," McKinsey & Company, mckinsey.com (April 27, 2017).

2. C. Lew, "How to Manage Effectively," knowyourteam.com (August 15, 2019).

3. J. Grenny, "How to Disagree with Your Boss," *Harvard Business Review*, hbr.org (November 2014).

5 Leading Those Who Report to You

Sure, as someone leading from the middle you get automatic influence over those who report to you because of your position power. But it's personal power well-wielded that separates the very best at effectively managing downward. The best at this know it's about relationships, not reporting lines. Their efforts yield commitment versus compliance. They know it's about being a facilitator, not a fixer, and that it's about helping others improve, not proving their own depth of knowledge.

All of that will be you after reading and putting into play this play-packed chapter. You'll learn how to become a once-in-a-career coach to your employees, how to have great coaching conversations, how to pinpoint their opportunity areas, how to give transformative feedback, and how to teach them in teachable moments.

So, let's get the growing going.

Have Great Coaching Conversations

Leading and influencing down in the organization starts with effective coaching, which centers on having effective coaching conversations. There are several types of coaching conversations, ranging from the initial role and expectation setting and relationship building discussion, to quick check-ins, to the formal performance review. Let's focus on where you can have the most influence on a continued basis, on ongoing developmental coaching conversations that take place during one-on-one meetings with your employees. The first step is to know how to structure these conversations. And that's where The Coaching Conversation Funnel comes in.

I've had more powerful coaching conversations than I can possibly recall using this model and have taught more to use it than I can hope to remember. Referring to Figure 5.1, the two funnels (one sitting on top of the other) are a visual reminder that every coaching conversation has a start and end that are very narrow and focused, with the middle of the conversation being where you really sit and expand discussion (denoted by the acronym SIT in Figure 5.1). Let's take a closer look.

Start: Don't just dive in and start talking in a coaching conversation. First, ensure the coachee has established a purpose and desired outcome to the discussion, otherwise you'll be tempted to insert yourself, drive the discussion, and skip to problem-solving. And nothing is more frustrating to a coachee than when you're giving them advice on something they don't need. Getting clear up front on the desired outcome of the session also forces the coachee to make choices about what they will talk about so that they can stay focused and accomplish what they set out to in the coaching conversation.

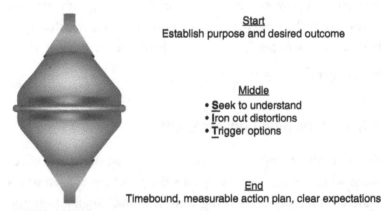

Start
Establish purpose and desired outcome

Middle
• Seek to understand
• Iron out distortions
• Trigger options

End
Timebound, measurable action plan, clear expectations

Figure 5.1 The Coaching Conversation Funnel

Source: hidesy/iStock/Getty Images

End: Far too many coaches just let a coaching conversation end without reinforcing expectations and accountability. Gallup research shockingly indicates that less than half of workers have a clear understanding of what's expected of them at work.[1] So take the opportunity at the end of each coaching conversation to drive clarity of expectations around what was discussed and to ensure the coachee feels accountable for the next steps. This helps drive action on the part of the coachee, which is where the transformational power of coaching lies.

Middle: As Figure 5.1 shows, the middle is where you SIT and spend most of your time during the coaching conversation. SIT is a handy acronym to remind you to conduct the middle part of the coaching conversation as follows.

- **S**eek to understand what your employee is saying or asking for help on. Use the probe, "Tell me more." Get at the real obstacle in their way by asking "What's the real challenge for you here?"

- **I**ron out distortions as well, meaning, know that sometimes the coachee will give a one-sided view of things, especially when it involves conflict with another person. (I've found that in these instances the truth usually lies somewhere in between your coachee's point of view and the other's point of view.) The point is to not let your coachee carry on with a distorted view of the situation they're describing. Bring your experience and perspective to the table to help them see the situation for what it really is.

- **T**rigger options for moving forward. That's a key part of your job as a coach, to keep things moving forward. You do that by entering the most critical part of the coaching conversation: when you guide versus prescribe. The art of doing so is laid out in Figure 5.2.

In regard to this spectrum, know that the heart of your coaching conversations will range from your using prescriptive language and actions to more guiding language and action. As a general rule of thumb, you want to be on the far-right side of this spectrum, in

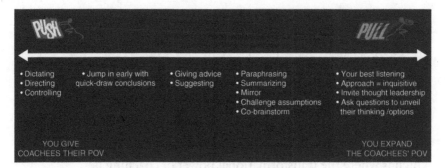

Figure 5.2 The Prescribe vs. Guide Spectrum

guiding mode. Referring to the right and left bottom corners of the figure, magic happens when you seek to expand the coachees' point of view, rather than give it to them, when you're engaging in more "pull" behaviors than "push" behaviors.

To illustrate, let's work our way from left to right on this spectrum.

When you dictate, direct, or control, coachees will be far less motivated to take action. Would you be more energized and committed to something your boss demanded you go do, or by something you discovered should be done? No contest. Now, there's a time to be on the far left of this spectrum, like during crisis or extreme adversity, when time and your experience is of the essence. In general, though, resist the far-left side.

Moving to the right, you're jumping into the conversation early with quick-draw conclusions (in your eagerness to move things forward faster). This is something I fell prey to too often as a younger coach. Farther right you're giving advice or making suggestions, both of which are fine, but realize that giving advice is not the same thing as coaching (a mistake new coaches often make). Advice giving is needed at times, but reserve it for after the coachees have had a chance to craft more of the "answer" on their own. As you move more toward the desired right side of the spectrum, you paraphrase and summarize what you heard to ensure understanding for you and your coachees. You serve as a mirror, helping them to understand how they're showing up and being perceived with their words and actions, and you co-brainstorm ideas and solutions together.

The far-right side, the true "pull" behaviors, is where the best coaching is. This is when you're listening at your peak ability (in fact you're doing 80 percent listening, 20 percent talking). Your approach comes off as inquisitive, in an attempt to understand and help, versus coming across like an inquisition, i.e. drilling coachees with questions and acting like a gate they have to get through. You invite the coachees' thought leadership, and you ask questions to unveil their thinking.

The key is to ask better questions.

When it comes to asking questions, the worst thing you can do is never ask. It's not much better when you ask leading questions. Asking close-ended questions is better than that, but best of all is to ask open-ended questions. To illustrate, let's say you wanted one of your product managers to consider taking a price increase on their product. Figure 5.3 outlines how you could approach this by asking different types of questions.

You quickly get a sense that just dictating to the product manager doesn't feel right, especially comparing to the other options. On the far right, where you ask an open-ended question, you can imagine that it empowers your employees to come up with their own solutions, broadening the scope of their thinking.

And that's how employees grow.

Bad			Good
FAILURE TO ASK	**LEADING QUESTIONS**	**CLOSED-ENDED QUESTIONS**	**OPEN-ENDED QUESTIONS**
"Take a price increase."	"Don't you think we should take a price increase?"	"Do you think we should take a price increase?"	"What should we do to offset our costs?"

Figure 5.3 Ask Better Questions

In Figure 5.4, you'll see lots of examples of open-ended questions you can ask throughout the Coaching Conversation Funnel.

Pinpoint Opportunity Areas

First and foremost, before we talk about spotting and articulating exactly how an employee can improve, be sure to celebrate, leverage, and build on their strengths. You get so much mileage and motivation out of doing so, yet so few managers start by strengthening someone's strengths before turning to their shortfalls. The instinct in many leaders is to start, and stay solely focused on, the latter.

That said, there comes a time when you owe it to your employees to help them improve on things that matter. With that in mind, consider this. Have you ever had someone working for you that you wanted to help improve, but you had a hard time pinpointing exactly what it was that they needed to work on? You knew they weren't as effective as they could be, and yet the exact issue eluded you.

Well, you aren't alone. One of the most common questions I field in the coaching arena is how to pinpoint one's performance opportunity area(s). And an opportunity area unidentified or misattributed is a missed opportunity for further personal growth at best, while at worst it has someone working on the wrong thing to improve. So, this can be a tricky endeavor, but it doesn't have to be. To guide you, just consider the prompts that follow—the six points of pinpointing opportunity areas.

1. 90 percent of the time opportunities lie in the shadow of strengths

When we excel at something, it can house an inverted downside. For example, someone who excels at creating and communicating a vision

Start

- What's the purpose of today's discussion?
- What outcome makes this discussion a success?
- What specifically do you want to achieve?
- What do you want to accomplish by when?
- How will you measure success?
- How much control do you have over attainment of this goal?

Middle

- What's happening in this situation? (seek to understand)
- Tell me more. What do you mean by that? (probe)
- You seem upset. What's behind that? (listen for emotion)
- What's your upset. What's behind that? (listen for emotion)
- How do you know that's accurate? (iron out distortions)
- This is what I heard you say; is that accurate? (mirror)
- What have you done to date about this? (reality check)
- What effect did that have? (reality check)
- What might be another way to look at that? (reframe)
- What could you do to change the situation? (trigger options)
- What options do you have? (trigger options)
- What approaches have worked in similar situations? (trigger options)
- What might be able to help? (trigger options)
- What action would make this a defining moment for you? (trigger options)
- How might you tackle that obstacle head-on? (trigger options)
- What fears/doubts are keeping you from moving forward? (trigger options)
- What would you try as a solution if you knew you wouldn't fail? (trigger options)
- What other resources could you draw from for a solution? (trigger options)

End

- What option is best for meeting your goal?
- What exactly will you commit to do now, by when?
- What are the success criteria and key milestones?
- Who needs to know what your plans are?
- What might get in the way and how will you overcome it?
- When can you share your progress with me?

Figure 5.4 Examples of Open-Ended Questions

may not be so good at following through on the level of detail required to carry that vision out. Or maybe someone who excels at attention to detail and thoroughness may not be very good at scoping up and setting a broad vision in a compelling, simple manner. Perhaps someone who's an outstanding collaborator isn't decisive enough for fear of not wanting to leave anyone's point of view behind. You get the idea. The hard-to-put-your-finger-on opportunity may well lie within juxtapositions like this.

2. Face reality

This is about being honest with yourself and the coachee and getting after the real area of opportunity. Sometimes we're kept from the hard truth because the truth is hard.

It's unpleasant when you're isolating an opportunity that is fairly fundamental to the success of the individual. Perhaps it's really not a style thing, but in fact it's insufficient leadership skills. Or maybe they don't just need to improve their communication, it's truly a quality of thinking issue. It just might be that they're fundamentally and arrogantly not valuing others, not just that they need to collaborate better.

The point is that great coaches can't let the difficulty and discomfort of seeing things clearly, and calling them true, actually blind them. Honesty and bravery are required to help others reach their true, and truly fulfilling, potential. In the end, I'd estimate at least 90 percent of those with whom you discuss a tough-to-hear opportunity area will ultimately appreciate hearing it, even if not right away. You owe your people the truth. And yes, being a great coach can sometimes mean helping your people move on from a job where your best assessment is that they won't succeed. Some of the most heartfelt appreciation I ever received came from an employee I coached out of the company and helped into another job/company that was a much better fit (and where he was soon thriving).

3. Discern between aptitude and attitude-based issues

To help pinpoint one's opportunity area and inform the necessary course of action, it's useful to ask yourself, "Is what they need to work on an attitude or aptitude issue?" To illustrate, suppose an employee is consistently producing inaccurate or untimely reports, important reports for the operation of the business. The poor performance could be coming from any number of underlying attitude issues. For example, perhaps they feel that the work is simply uninteresting, that someone else should be doing it, that there's no positive consequence for doing it, they think something else is more important, or they're rewarded in some way for not doing it. The result is an all too nonchalant attitude toward the task and very indifferent, dispassionate behavior in general.

With all this in mind, you could reframe tasks for employees, show them the importance of the reports, indicate how they'll be rewarded for doing the work well, explain how they're uniquely suited to do it, and discuss the undesired behaviors behind the attitude. Any number of tactics could be employed to help coachees see the task differently and trigger a more favorable underlying attitude and set of corresponding behaviors.

Now let's say you discover that the poor performance is aptitude based. For example, you find that the employee never got training on the reports, so they don't actually know what they're supposed to do, how or when to do it, or why they're doing it. Or it might be that they actually think they're already doing it correctly. This scenario requires some fundamental skill building to enable people to do the work with success.

The point is that behaviors and outcomes that have attitudinal issues at their core trigger the need for one set of actions. Those that have a deficient skillset at the core require another. Pinpoint which of the two is at work and adjust your approach accordingly.

4. Isolate the "one-offs" and look for themes

We can all screw things up on occasion. As a coach trying to pinpoint an opportunity area for growth, however, you're looking for themes, not "one-off" misses. Newer coaches often assume one observation of an undesired behavior equals a theme. Not necessarily. So, don't be distracted by a singular event, unless it is symptomatic of some underlying theme you're observing.

5. Calibrate your point of view for accuracy

Once you've pinpointed the opportunity areas at hand, or even if you're still in the hypothesis stage, it's a good idea to solicit input from informed outsiders. To do so, establish what I call a "Personal Board of Directors" for the coachee. Select a few people who interact with the coachee, but who do so from a much more observational and "elevated" point of view. For example, for a brand manager, enroll the VP of Research, the Director of Finance, and the Director of Sales as "board members" (or any more senior positions that get opportunities to see the brand manager in action on occasion). Their role on the board is to assist you by observing the brand manager from an informed distance, and offering perspective on performance accordingly. Their at-arm's-length, yet experienced, point of view can offer another source of pinpointing insight and tends to be amazingly accurate, even if based on only a few observations. Furthermore, they've probably seen more than one brand manager, maybe even in the same role, and can offer calibrating and comparative insight as well. Leverage this seasoned input as you home in on opportunity areas (and strengths) as an aid to your own judgment.

6. Get the skeletons out of their closet

Some of the best pinpointing comes straight from coachees themselves. If you've built up a foundation of trust, you can ask them, "What aren't you good at that you don't want anyone to know about?" (i.e. their "skeletons"). Odds are, if they don't want anyone to know about it, it's something really important, maybe even fundamental, to them being able to succeed in their job.

For example, maybe they don't understand a profit-and-loss statement, they don't feel comfortable in customer calls, they don't like speaking in front of groups, or they feel they have weak analytical skills. Not easy things to admit, but if you can get your coachees to open up and help you pinpoint their skeletons, you can put together a plan to help them get better at essential skills in a safe environment. Strike an agreement that if they'll come clean, you won't judge them for it. You'll just help catapult them past it. Keep the opportunity "off paper" (i.e. not part of any formal performance review) and between you and your coachee only. It's a tremendous way to influence your employees in a positive way that they won't soon forget.

With the six points of pinpointing considered, let's move on to the tricky task of giving highly effective feedback.

Give Transformative Feedback

Gallup regularly conducts State of the Workplace studies and they keep confirming a hard to swallow truth. Seventy percent of employees don't agree with the statement "In the last six months, someone has talked to me about my progress."[2]

The truth is, many employees really don't know how well (or not) they're performing. And it's not just the quantity of feedback given that's lacking, unfortunately, it's also the quality. Gallup data also shows that only 26 percent of employees agree that the feedback they receive always helps them do their work better.[3] In fact, an analysis of 131 studies on feedback effectiveness found that in more than one-third of the cases where it was possible to assess the effectiveness of feedback, providing feedback actually *hurt* subsequent performance.[4]

Yikes.

Maybe this will make you feel better: I'd argue we're all genetically pre-programmed to be poor at giving feedback, especially corrective feedback. After all, who likes pointing out others' shortcomings to them? We instinctively want to sugarcoat it, which often results in our being unclear. Or we want to be clear and end up being too brittle and spur defensiveness. Or we might approach giving feedback too casually, without enough preparation, and end up coming across as undervaluing or insincere.

And that's a shame because giving feedback is one of the most powerful moments of influence that you have. But not to worry, here are the eight fundamentals of feedback; follow these to excel in this space.

1. Be specific

Giving feedback in broad strokes, without being specific and using examples, nets confusion and frustration. And just saying "Great job!" without details makes it less meaningful. Good feedback versus bad is like whole grain versus white bread. The former is granular, infused with flavor and wholesomeness, the latter is generic, bland, and far from nutritious.

2. Be sincere

If you're praising someone, put heartfelt emotion into it. If it's corrective feedback, show it's well-intended and meant to help them grow. If it comes from the heart, it sticks in the mind.

3. Be calibrating

Provide context, especially with corrective feedback. For example, say you give feedback on what could have gone better during a sales presentation. Deep down, employees receiving this information will wonder if that kind of feedback is typical at this stage of their career or if it's a sign that they're off track. Without context, employees assume the worst. So, clarify, letting them know the corrective opportunity is to be expected at this stage of their career, or telling them it signals that they're "off-track" regarding their development and career aspirations.

4. Be proportionate

Don't overstate or understate what you're praising or pushing on. And remember that we do far more right than wrong as human beings, and want to be reminded as such. Keep the distribution of feedback proportionate with this reality—my experience and a variety of research shows a 5:1 ratio is ideal (five pieces of positive feedback for every corrective one).

5. Be timely

Related to the above, waiting too long to share feedback drastically dilutes its value. After-the-fact feedback means matter of fact (i.e. it won't have an impact). It can even cause resentment, making the giver seem lazy and uncaring.

6. Be tailored

When it comes to receiving feedback, my experience is that we all fall into one of three categories. First, those who want the harder-to-hear stuff right up front; they can't enjoy positive reinforcement until they hear the corrective feedback (that's me). Second, those who want the "compliment sandwich" (good followed by bad then good again). Third, those who claim they want the first, but really want the second. Find out preferences by asking.

7. Beware of feedback traps

Besides failing to deliver on the fundamentals above, what follows are the biggest mistakes well-meaning managers make when giving feedback.

Giving feedback too infrequently. Don't save feedback for the annual performance review. Share it early and often. How often depends on the willingness and needs of the individual. Stay on the more frequent side if in doubt.

Bringing others in. In general, when giving feedback, don't take the easy way out and just share what others have said. What do *you* feel or see? What do *you* have to say about the situation? Use others' opinions as a sounding board as discussed earlier (i.e. the Personal Board of Directors), but feedback must come from you. You're the conductor here, not a conduit.

Lack of bravery. You owe your employees the truth. It's that simple. And that hard.

Making it about the individual, not the action. Corrective feedback should be about the employee and his or her behaviors and actions, never about them as a human being.

Guessing at motives. Don't guess at why the person engaged in the behavior or action you're giving them feedback on. Stay focused on the impact of both.

Wrong setting. Keep corrective feedback private and don't be afraid to praise in public (if the employee likes to be publicly praised).

Too much sugarcoating. This is a natural tendency because everyone wants to be nice. But you must get to the point, without masking it. The longer you take to spit it out, the more frustrating and confusing it is. Avoid mixed messages. Which brings us to the next one.

Backtracking at the end. I used to do this. In a deep-seated desire to end things well, at the end of the feedback session, I'd unintentionally water down the corrective feedback I just gave, causing confusion. Stick to your guns. End on a supportive, but clear, note that reinforces the feedback you just gave.

Not being prepared. You owe the employee your clearest, most concise comments, which won't surface if you haven't thought the feedback through in advance.

Making it one-way. Employees want a chance to respond to your feedback. Give them that opportunity and check for clarity, comprehension, and commitment.

Failing to document. Sometimes you need a paper trail to justify a decision. It's not fun making notes on what was discussed, but it's good foresight.

8. Follow a framework

Now, even with knowing all of the feedback traps, it can still be uncomfortable when it comes right down to actually having the feedback conversation. I combed through the most successful, commonly used frameworks for giving feedback and combined it with my own insight having coached (and taught others to coach) for three decades. The result is the powerful framework that follows, built on the acronym SHARES. It's built with the need to give corrective feedback in mind, but it works just as well for giving positive feedback. Follow this step-by-step framework to share feedback in a way that will have the influence you intend.

Situation. First, give context on the feedback you're going to give by describing the situation that surrounds it. Stick to the facts without emotion, especially if you're giving tough feedback to a difficult employee. It's easy to get the feedback session off to a horrendous start by allowing your frustration or anger to show through. It automatically puts the recipient in self-defense mode.

Halo. Now that you've set the context, you can halo the discussion with empathy, sincerity, and a clear intent to offer support. Receiving tough feedback is hard to hear no matter who you are, so the recipient deserves humanity and grace. That said, be firm, especially with the difficult employee.

Articulate. Give specific details on the performance issue (or thing you're praising). Know that difficult underperformers often use the lack of specificity and clarity of prior feedback as an excuse for why the undesirable behavior has continued. Don't let them off the hook.

Result. Share the result or impact that the behavior or outcome is having on you, others, a project, or even the employee's desired career progression. And especially with difficult employees, it's important to be crystal clear on the consequences of them not addressing the performance issue satisfactorily.

Example. Give an example of an alternative behavior or desired outcome (or an example of the exact behavior you're looking to positively reinforce). This goes to the need for specificity and clarity again; it's critical that employees understand what good looks like here. And especially for difficult underperformers, it's important to let them choose the solutions for arriving at the desired alternative behavior/outcome. You want the employee feeling like they're an empowered part of the solution, not like they've had an ultimatum dictated to them.

Solicit. Ask for the employee's point-of-view while listening to understand and empathize. Understand that if it was difficult-to-hear feedback, the employee may be experiencing shock or anger. They may feel rejected or want to reject what was said. Or they might move quickly into acceptance and feelings of embarrassment or extreme humility. Give the employee space to process. Be comfortable with silence. Close firm, but supportive.

By the way, for the toughest feedback for the hardest to work with employees, even before you launch into the SHARES method, you can open your feedback session with what I call The Golden Question. Ask the employee, "How do you think you're doing?" You might be surprised at how self-aware your difficult employee is. They may bring up some of the toughest things you wanted to cover, thus softening the blow, or at least give you a less abrupt, gentler way in to broach the topic.

If they are hopelessly not self-aware, just go right into the SHARES method. But as you do, remember what happens in the case of desert farming. In arid parts of the world, farmers use a series of long, thin tubes with tiny holes in them to slowly drip water onto plants underneath. If they didn't control the flow of water and it came out too fast, the water would just collect and sit on the sunbaked surface, evaporating before it could be absorbed.

So it is when employees are flooded with too much corrective feedback all at once. They can't absorb it all, it sits on the surface and then just evaporates into thin air, without sinking in. So, talk through one issue at a time, walking through the SHARES model for each piece of corrective feedback before moving on to the next one in your feedback discussion.

The bottom line here is that if you stick to all of these fundamentals, you'll make your feedback a gift, not a grudge.

Teach in Teachable Moments

There are brief windows in time when an employee is particularly pliable to learning something new or when the time is disproportionately ripe for a lesson to be taught and to have it stick. These are called teachable moments and the very best of those who lead from the middle are tuned into when these moments arise. You've already got so much to focus on, so here's help to prevent you from missing some of the most common teachable moments. When you spot one of these nine points in time, don't pass up the opportunity to invest and influence.

1. When reality doesn't match expectations

I believe in a simple equation: Happiness = Reality − Expectations. The equation goes negative, and unhappiness in the manager/employee relationship arises, when what's happening in reality falls beneath expectations. In these moments, ensure the employee is clear on the reality of what they're delivering or how they're behaving and that they understand what you're expecting. Provide the guidance they need to help them get back to meeting or exceeding those expectations.

2. When they're seeing things from just their side during conflicts

I mentioned earlier in this chapter that when it comes to interpretations of a conflict between two sides, the truth usually lies somewhere in the middle. A classic telltale teachable moment occurs when one of the parties can only see things from his or her point of view. In these moments, help your employee to step back and objectively consider the opposing point of view. It strengthens the outcome, resolves conflict faster, and stretches the muscle that enables employees to see the bigger picture.

3. When the "A" game isn't present in an "A" situation

"A" situations can include big meetings, pivotal points in a project's life, or a crisis, just to name a few. The lack of "A" game might show up as a highly flawed recommendation, a lack of anticipating questions or pushbacks, poor delivery of key messages, a lack of urgency or proactivity, or any other number of ways in which less than optimal performance showed up in high stakes situations. Don't miss the chance to instruct here on an important teachable moment.

4. When someone falls short on a risk taken

Proceed carefully here, teachers-in-waiting. The point is not to discourage risk-taking, but to encourage more of it. Help the risk-takers learn where they went wrong, what they could have done better to avoid the outcome, or what will make the next venture more successful—and do so in an uplifting, encouraging manner. A study found that 41 percent of employees said their manager never encouraged them to take risks while another 33 percent said their manager only sometimes encouraged them to take risks.[5]

While you're at it, clarify the rules of risk-taking. What constitutes a good risk? A bad one? What happens if the employee succeeds in taking a risk? Fails? Who needs to approve the risk to be taken? You get the point. When employees are clear on the rules of risk-taking, they're far more likely to engage in doing so, which is what any innovation-driven, continual-improvement-seeking leader in the middle would want. By the way, nothing is stopping you from getting clear with your boss on what the rules of risk-taking are for you, either. If you don't know, ask.

5. When they're not aware of the perception/impression they're leaving

Every once in a while we all need a mirror held up in front of ourselves. Note that this is a teachable moment, not a preachable moment. The idea is not to lecture your employees on being more like you, or to have perfect behavior in all situations. This is merely a powerful opportunity to give coachees the gift of insight through introspection. Help them understand how they're showing up, and then help them connect the dots to how they really want to show up. Too many would rather complain about the net impact of someone's behavior rather than help them to see the impact that the behavior is having on its recipients.

6. When you have the chance to share the view from the window seat

Teachable moments can arise when you've had an experience your employees don't ordinarily have access to, and then you choose to share it with them. For example, perhaps you just got back from a leadership summit where interesting, important, and relevant things took place. Take the time to download the experience with your team. Or maybe you just spent time with the CEO and got the chance to see how they think, feel, and act. Share your observations with your direct reports. Sharing the view from the window seat helps people see "what it's like" and presents a great learning opportunity.

7. When you see gaps in preparation or thinking

As responsible managers, especially in the middle, when we spot gaps we often instinctively just fill them in. But doing so too quickly can mean a teachable moment is bypassed, especially when it comes to gaps in preparation or thinking. In such times, point out to coachees exhibiting this shortfall where they could have been better prepared or what could have been thought through more, and why. Doing so will improve the completeness of their efforts moving forward and help them more completely develop.

8. When you spell out the difference between good and great

This is closely related to aligning on expectations, but deserves its own point. Quite often, people don't deliver great simply because they don't know what great looks like. I've found it to be an incredibly powerful teaching moment when you sit down with coachees and literally spell out the difference between good and great. As I shared in *Find the Fire*, create a simple grid with three columns. The first column contains the performance vectors that count most at your company (for example, thinking and problem solving, vision, or initiative and follow-through). In the second column, you spell out, in writing, what good performance looks like for each of those performance variables. In the third column, you spell out, in writing, what great performance looks like for each variable.

Investing the time to do this and talk it through with coachees will do two things. First, it sets clear expectations for what great performance looks like on as many variables as you want to discuss. Second, it leads to individualized learning plans. For example, after having the good-to-great discussion, an employee might learn that to deliver on what's considered great thinking and problem solving, they'll need to get training on certain things. Presto—an individualized learning plan is born.

The point is, having this discussion leads to many powerful moments of learning and improved performance. After all, very few people aren't interested in being great, especially when they clearly understand what great looks like.

9. When tempers are lost or excuses are made

Finally, teachable moments lie in the times when employees don't own the moment in which they react poorly—particularly when they lose their temper or make excuses. While there may be plenty of instances where losing one's temper is justified, it's rarely productive and presents an opportunity for reflection. What was at the root cause of the outburst? How much of it can coachees own to prevent such tension in the future?

The same applies to excuse-making. Coachees will benefit from seeing how unbecoming it is, and in being honest with themselves about how much of the outcome they own (thus learning, improving, and preventing the need for excuses in the future).

So, you've learned how to lead and influence powerfully up and down your organization; now it's time to go across in the next few chapters.

Notes:

1. B. Rigoni and B. Nelson, "Do Employees Really Know What's Expected of Them?" *Gallup Business Journal*, news.gallup.com (September 27, 2016).

2. "Gallup 2017 State of the American Workplace," gallup.com/workplace.

3. J. Clifton and J. Harter, "It's the Manager," Gallup Press, p. 154 (May 2019).

4. A.S. DiNisi and A.N. Kluger, "Feedback Effectiveness: Can 360 Degree Feedback Be Improved?" *The Academy of Management Executive* 14, no. 1 (February 2000): 129–139.

5. "Employee Engagement Research Report," blessingwhite.com (January 2013).

6 Leading Teams

Your influence multiplies exponentially from the middle when you lead a team with excellence, which is a specialty skill you can develop. You'll do just that in this chapter, armed with multiple specialty tools.

The first of these tools is based on an important insight. If you want to be great at leading teams, the most direct way is to understand what great teams look like; how they feel, how they act, and what their norms are. Know what signs mark a truly great team, and then do what it takes to replicate those signs showing up on your team, too.

Signs That You're Leading Your Team Exceptionally Well

Here are the 15 telltale signs of the most successful teams, based on decades of research and observation across teams of all kinds, in business, sports, non-profits, education, and more. If you can already spot these signs, you're leading teams from the middle with mastery. For those signs you don't see yet, you'll get help to make them materialize and make your team even better.

1. Psychological safety is abundant

Google spent several years studying what makes great teams great. They concluded that the single most important factor was the presence of psychological safety: not being afraid to take risks in front of the team, no fear of getting rejected for putting yourself and your opinions and ideas out there, feeling able to bring your whole self to work.[1]

If your team isn't there yet on this front, role model the way. Commend versus condemn others for their mistakes and opposing point of view. Invite people in to contribute and reward them when they do. Shut down any signs of one employee disrespecting another. Back up a team member when you see them getting knocked down—when they're repeatedly cut off while trying to make a point, when they're getting unfairly berated by another manager or savaged when they're not in the room. Stand out by standing up for them and showing that a safe environment is non-negotiable.

2. There's a zero-complacency policy

Fueled by psychological safety, the most successful teams take collective risks and collectively accept the blame if something goes wrong. They're uncomfortable with the status quo and have a mindset of continual improvement and growth. They can't stand to sit still.

If you see signs of complacency versus the opposite, dial up the external focus. Paint a clear picture of your competitor's capabilities and strategies. Share industry trends that illuminate the need for change. You can also empower and challenge your team more. Grant more autonomy than makes you feel comfortable while upping accountability for hitting goals. Share stories of how complacency has hurt your company in the past to further dial up discomfort with the status quo and a sense of urgency.

3. Decisions are debated, made, then committed to

Despite common belief, the most successful teams debate. A lot. Especially when everyone feels psychologically safe to share their point of view. (For help on fostering healthy debate, recall that Chapter 2 covers this.) But then debate halts and the decision is made, after which everyone commits to the decision *as if it were their own.*

It's up to the team leader, of course, to be decisive. If that's you, don't let emotions or perfectionism keep you from making decisions. Further aid your decisiveness by stepping back and evaluating the true impact of a wrong decision (which often isn't that dire) or what the risk is of not deciding. Set timebound parameters for making the call and avoid rehashing the same set of data and experiences, instead seeking fresh perspective to help accelerate the decision. Revisit what you're trying to accomplish with the decision to be made; doing so might suddenly illuminate a clear choice among a set of options.

Finally, make it clear that once the decision is made, commitment, not just grumbling compliance, is expected. As an example, a very successful team leader I interviewed credited her team's success to the three-word mantra emblazoned on a wall-to-wall poster hanging in the team meeting room: "Debate. Decide. Commit."

4. You hear "we" more than "me"

Team leaders of the most successful teams continually reinforce the importance of team goals over individual goals. The team's priorities are everyone's priorities. That said, individual problems are everyone's problem, as the best teams rally around and support one another.

If you don't hear enough "we," keep going back to the team's goals and keep rewarding team accomplishments. Much in this list will also naturally create a greater sense of unity.

5. Everyone knows their role (and everyone else's role) on the "assembly line"

If you want a high-performing team, it's absolutely vital that everyone on the team understands exactly what their role is and what they're expected to contribute to the team. Each team member should also know the role their fellow team members play and respect that role, looking for opportunities to invite each other in for support and assistance.

Here's a solve if you're not seeing this. Hold an all-hands-on-deck team meeting to educate on this topic. Have each team member describe their role, how they see themselves fitting into the team, including what strengths they bring to the team. You'd be surprised how few teams do this and just how helpful it can be for establishing a baseline of understanding and respect for one another. The next level of this occurs in the next item on this list.

6. A sense of interdependence underlies everything

This is more than just a feeling of "we," more than knowing everyone's role on the team. This is a feeling of fierce commitment to one another. A sense of mutual accountability and the belief that every team member can depend on the others without fail.

You can drive a greater sense of interdependency by setting expectations for specific interdependent behavior. For example, encourage team members to share their expertise and information, to raise their hand and own failure while pointing their finger at others with success, to operate with unswerving honesty and transparency, and to seek each other out for help and support. I've even created a document for a client that I call a "Declaration of Interdependence" (playing on the famous American document), a version of a team charter that lists team goals, deliverables, role definitions, and behavioral expectations for all team members to adhere to.

7. Adversity and stress bring the team closer together, not further apart

The character of any great team (or team leader) is revealed in times of adversity and stress. When the underlying team bond is strong, each team member instinctively wants to unite and support one another when things get tough.

To strengthen this sense, never waste a crisis. The next time your team faces adversity, role model calmness and decisiveness to help pull everyone together and make clear the behavior you expect. In fact, whenever I took over as a team leader somewhere, I'd share a document with the team titled, "In Times of Adversity." It spelled out the leadership behaviors they could expect from me when things got difficult. How you act in adversity can help bring the team closer together, or not, and the impressions you leave will be lasting ones (whether good or bad). So make it count.

8. There's a sense of "relaxed intensity"

This term means having a very intentional balance of the seriousness and commitment it takes to win with the camaraderie and fun it takes to win *on a sustained basis*. Perhaps more than any other item on this list, this sense is set by the team leader.

If you show nothing but intensity 24/7, you'll burn out your team. That doesn't mean you abandon your intensity as a leader, it's still very much there. You express it more thoughtfully, blending it with empathy, emotional intelligence, and a heavy dose of just wanting to have fun. Laughter is as important as lambasting competition. So, while you're pushing hard and heavy with your team for great results, lighten up.

9. Positive gossip only

This is a subtler sign, but an important one nonetheless. There is simply no room for negativity and backstabbing on great teams. In fact, on the best teams, team members find opportunities to talk positively about one another, in genuine ways.

If you see violations here, shut them down. Immediately. Never get caught talking negatively about a team member yourself.

Nothing sends the message that doing so is okay more than when the team leader is seen doing it. Do the opposite, find ways to give public praise for individual efforts (while always first emphasizing the team's goals and accomplishments). Create a process for team members to be able to give peer-to-peer recognition. Talk up a new team member before they arrive on the team and honor them when it's time for them to leave the team.

10. Ownership is everywhere

On the most successful teams, you never hear anyone saying, "Not my square." Stepping up to contribute even beyond one's role is the norm. And when something goes wrong, people are falling over each other to take the blame.

If you instead spot pockets of a lack of accountability, restate your expectations on this front and spell out the consequences of a lack of ownership behavior. Know that a lack of ownership often comes from someone feeling like they won't be rewarded for the extra effort it requires. So, reinforce that while team goals are the priority, individual efforts and accomplishments certainly won't go unrecognized.

11. Team members invest in one another

They take the time and effort to get to know and support each other. They're careful to be inclusive. They celebrate together, and enjoy giving peer-to-peer recognition where they celebrate each other.

If your team's personalities aren't fully gelling, or if there's too much avoidance of one another versus investment, it's quite likely they really haven't taken the time to establish relationships with each other. You can help this along by creating purposeful bonding experiences. For example, coordinate celebrations of success or failures or gatherings just to have fun. Or give the team the chance to solve a tough problem together. Working together to crack a problem and fulfill a mission creates a shared sense of identity, which draws teams closer together and encourages sacrifices for one another. As does pulling teams together to work in a crucible moment, like making a big decision or setting a big vision together.

12. The right things are communicated

Great teams also invest in the hard work of communicating with one another. They take the time to share key information to help progress the mission but also just to help each other learn. Feedback is freely given and accepted in the right spirit.

When teams are operating poorly, it can often be traced back to poor communication. You can change that by investing heavily in the hard work of communication yourself. Set the standard, and the expectations, on this front. Formalize what you want communicated and the channels you want used, if necessary. And get practiced at giving and openly asking for feedback. Make it a part of the culture.

13. Transparency and truth reign

No team can operate at anywhere near its peak level without transparency and truth as a standard operating procedure. Period. Nothing is more transparent than when someone is not being transparent, so team members will notice breaches from each other on this front. And just one occasion of dishonesty is all it takes to break the chain of camaraderie, forever.

This is one place for you to have a zero-tolerance policy. The team must operate on a bedrock of truth and candor with one another. Executing the entirety of this list well will put the building blocks of truth and trust in place for your team. Then it's about your unwavering demand that this be a core operating norm.

14. Optimism and confidence are a default

The best teams exude self-belief and the belief that great things are coming. Negativity from any team member stands out like a sore thumb.

The biggest enabler you can provide here is to help team members feel self-confident and stay positive. To foster self-confidence in others, remind them to stop comparing themselves to others, and that the only comparison that matters is to who they were yesterday and whether or not they're becoming a better version of themselves. Get them focused on their potential, not their limitations. Help them learn from failures and to accept that perfection is an empty pursuit.

To counter pockets of negativity, highlight the impact the negativity is having on others (and redirect energy toward positivity). And know that cynics get their power when no one challenges them. Invite the cynics to offer solutions instead. If they can't, they lose their power.

15. Purpose is on a pedestal

The best teams work with a clear, compelling, and catalyzing sense of purpose. They leverage that sense of purpose above all else to keep them on track and motivated toward their mission and goals.

It's such an important part of what makes great teams great, something you can so clearly spearhead for your team, that I saved it for last on this list. And it's why we'll spend extra time enabling you on this front in what follows.

Galvanizing a Team Around Purpose

A team working with a strong sense of purpose is a force to be reckoned with. And as the team leader, one of the most potent tools you have for catalyzing a team is to instill a sense of purpose to the work the team does. Purpose is the profound "Why"—Why are you working so hard and spending so much time away from loved ones? For what higher order reason? Most leaders in the middle have heard or read about purpose, and perhaps how it can be applied at the company or individual level. But advice on how to create and apply it tends to lack specificity, staying at the conceptual level. It thus produces the reaction, "Sure, nice idea. But what am I supposed to do with it?" And the typical advice doesn't address how to specifically create a sense of purpose at the team level.

Let's change all of this right now.

The truth is, one of the very first places employees turn to for a sense of purpose in their life is to their work, their company. Within that, the most meaning comes from an employee's membership in a team, their work family. That's why crafting a purpose for your team is so powerful. When a team is working with a clear sense of purpose, it gives them something to return to when they feel lost. It helps provide direction, clarity of intent, and informs how they should think, act, and feel and for what higher order reason. It helps the team forge a powerful collective identity.

It's for all these reasons that I introduce you to The Purpose Pyramid (see Figure 6.1), a tool I've used many times on my own businesses and that I've helped many companies successfully leverage for theirs. It helps you articulate your team's sense of purpose and spells out how to leverage that purpose to produce real results. (It can be used at the company level too.)

So, let's dive in.

To walk you through how this tool works, I'll share a case study from my work as team leader of one of the most important new product launches in Procter & Gamble history, the Prilosec OTC launch (a treatment for frequent heartburn). At the time of the launch in 2003, Prilosec was the largest selling prescription drug on the

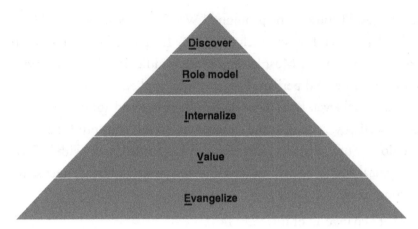

Figure 6.1 The Purpose Pyramid

planet. Its patent was expiring, and P&G had won the right to take the product over the counter. It would be the biggest Rx-to-OTC switch in history. So, we knew it would be a project for the Prilosec team that would be ripe with purpose. If only we could harness it. Enter the Purpose Pyramid. The pyramid is encapsulated in an easy to remember acronym, DRIVE, as in this is how you specifically create a sense of purpose and drive it down through and across your team for maximum effect. Let's take it one step, one letter, at a time.

Discover. The first step is to discover your team's purpose, not invent it, because chances are it already exists. Ask the *why, who,* and *what* questions. Talk to your longest standing team members or customers of that team and ask them *why* the team was formed to do what they do. For what higher order reason? How can you find common ground on higher ground? Ask *who* does your team ultimately serve, and how? Ask *what* can your team be the absolute best at? Enroll your entire team in these questions so they're a part of creating the purpose, not just recipients of it.

As a bonus question, you can also ask what your team's most closely held values are. A team living their values with great intention every day is a great starting point, or even a proxy, for a purpose.

With all of this as fodder, you'll identify threads of what your team's purpose might be. Pick a thread that feels most pertinent and powerful and then boil it down to a simple sentence. On Prilosec, we had a spirit of asking each other "Have we asked for enough?," enough of ourselves, of our customers. It led to the purpose statement for the Prilosec team: "Set the gold standard to give the gold standard." Meaning, we knew we had to set the bar for the company with this launch given how important it was for the company. And we had to protect the entire product experience for the consumer as we brought it over the counter (it was the gold standard treatment for a debilitating condition).

As you develop your own team's purpose statement, how do you know if it's a good one? One simple filter. Ask this question about your draft purpose statement: *Is it definitive about the difference you're thrilled to make?* If it is, magic.

Role model. Having discovered your team's purpose, now it's time to role model it. Sure, roll the purpose into your team's behaviors and vernacular—that's the obvious part. But I'm talking here about leveraging the purpose statement to actually help you make decisions. *Use it to keep reminding yourself of what you're fighting for.* That's another filter, by the way. If the purpose statement inspires the thought of what you're fighting for and reenergizes you to keep fighting for it, it's a good one.

Keep the purpose statement in front of your team, even if you have to print it, frame it, and bring it into team meetings with you. On Prilosec, many times decisions were made based on the reminding thought, "Will this decision help us set the gold standard to give the gold standard?" Thus, the purpose statement even helped us make the right decision.

Internalize. Employees have to internalize how the purpose comes to life in their jobs. If they don't make the connection, it's just a meaningless sentence painted on the team meeting room wall or in the main lobby of HQ. Nothing will be done with it nor will it inspire any behavior change. Challenge team members to articulate how the purpose specifically comes to life in their jobs. For example, a grocery chain I keynoted for held essay contests, offering a $500 prize to employees who wrote the best articulations of how their job supported the company purpose. You get the idea. If needed, sit down with each team member and help them draw the connection between their work and the team's purpose.

Value. With everyone fully enrolled now, it's time to walk the talk even more by visibly demonstrating that you value adherence to the purpose. This is where you reward behaviors consistent with upholding the purpose. Create a fund for the leadership team members (for the head of sales, product development, marketing, etc.) to use at their discretion to recognize and reward team members when they're seen acting in accordance with the team's purpose.

Evangelize. Finally, enroll passionate change agents, team members especially excited about the purpose and eager to help others embrace it. Give all team members, especially those on the front line, tools to help encourage the evangelizing of the purpose. For example, provide a budget for everyone (not just the leadership team) that they can pull from to reward each other with tokens of appreciation on the spot for behavior they see that exemplifies the purpose.

Having your team working with a deep sense of purpose will make a massive difference. When Prilosec OTC launched in 2003, *Advertising Age* named it the number-three most successful product launch of the year, in any category. For perspective, number one that year was this little thing called the Apple iPod, second was the Schick Quatro razor (which kicked off the multi-blade razor wars). The brand achieved its entire first year sales goal in *five days*, immediately catapulted to a leadership position in the heartburn category, broke multiple company sales records, and to this day is considered one of the most successful brand launches in company history. And a well-articulated sense of purpose was our fuel.

Shaping How Employees Experience Your Leadership Team

One of the most important teams you'll ever run as someone leading from the middle is your leadership team—the group of (usually) six to ten people or so that you partner with most closely to guide decisions, many of whom are likely at or close to your hierarchical level. The leadership team is how many employees experience "upper management," like when they come into a leadership team meeting to present progress on an initiative or to get input on an issue. It's in these occasions that leadership teams build an important reputation that can motivate, or demotivate, the troops, based on the way they interact with the employees. The experience employees have with the leadership team heavily influences "the smell of the place."

I've worked with many leadership teams to get them to think of themselves as a brand. Much like a brand has an equity (what it stands for, what differentiates it, what the consumer/user experiences when engaging with the brand), so does a leadership team. What follows is a tool to help you and your leadership team be intentional about the impression you're making on the constituents you interact with, to be mindful of the experience they have. It's another pyramid, but of a different kind.

Figure 6.2 demonstrates how this pyramid works, using a real-world example from my experience. Let's walk through it.

Leadership Team (LT) Desired Equity: The top of this pyramid is the net impression you want employees to have about your leadership team. In the example, this particular leadership team wanted to leave employees feeling that: "We help make every project better and leave every employee feeling supported." The leadership team reviewed this Desired Equity before every leadership team meeting to help remind them of the behaviors to show in that meeting (especially if employee "guests" were on the agenda).

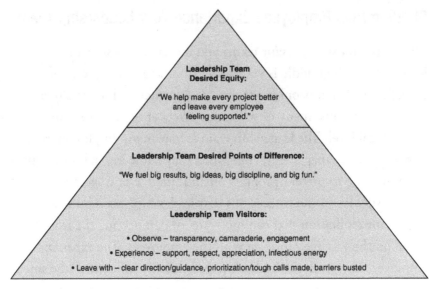

Figure 6.2 The Leadership Team Equity Pyramid

LT Desired Points of Difference: This is where the leadership team decides, very specifically, how they want to stand out from other teams. This leadership team decided they wanted to differentiate themselves as such: "We fuel big results, big ideas, big discipline, and big fun." Adhering to this made the team stand out within the company, big time.

LT Visitors: Here, the leadership team members imagined the exact experience they wanted employees (visitors to leadership team meetings) to have. They wanted visitors to:

- Observe: transparency, camaraderie, engagement

- Experience: support, respect, appreciation, infectious energy

- Leave With: clear direction and guidance, prioritization/tough calls made, barriers busted

Your leadership team has a disproportionate impact on the competency and culture of your workplace. So, be intentional with the power it wields by working with your leadership team to craft your own equity pyramid.

Setting Powerful Team Goals

An often-overlooked source of team excellence is goal setting. To think of the opportunity here, think of the opposite. Ever been issued a dull goal, filled with gigantic numbers sourced from ludicrous assumptions, absent of any heart? Right. You can recall how motivated you felt to achieve that goal (i.e. not at all). Now think of a time when you were working toward a goal that had great personal meaning to you, the achievement of which truly mattered. The difference in discretionary energy you expend on achieving these two kinds of goals is extraordinary.

So how do you set team goals that motivate versus deflate or that are ignored? First, I offer the best of classical team goal setting advice to make any goal you set intrinsically motivating. That is, ensure it's a common goal that unites the team and supersedes individual goals or what each function is rewarded for (sales is typically rewarded differently than product supply, for example). Make the goal compelling so that it's clear what's in it for the employees and so that it connects with them personally and emotionally. Such goals create energy on their own and draw people to them.

Now, for the non-standard advice.

The Three Zones Test

To ensure each goal you're setting will be effective, conduct the Three Zones Test. That is, ask yourself one question regarding the goal you're about to set: "Does this goal push employees out of their *comfort* zone, but not to the *danger* zone, such that it shines in the *twilight* zone?"

An explanation is in order. Great goals consider three zones. They're stretching enough to take a team out of their *comfort* zone, so complacency has no chance of settling in. The goal should be challenging enough that only the team working as a unit could accomplish it.

That said, the goals should be grounded in reality, based on assumptions that you at least have a line-of-sight to achieving. In other words, they don't push a team into a *danger* zone of being so unrealistic as to be depressing or to force unscrupulous behaviors to actually achieve.

Finally, imagine your employees in the twilight of their career (near the end)—what I call the *twilight* zone (a wink to a popular, old American TV show). If they were asked to look back on their time with your team and reflect upon accomplishment of the goals you set, would they feel achieving those goals was something worthy and memorable? If achieving the goal meets the standard of creating pride upon reflection, it's a darn good goal.

Team goals don't have to be afterthoughts anymore. They can inspire your team to put on the afterburners.

Influencing Team Behavior in Times of Poor Results

Plenty can and has been said about leading teams in times of business crisis. The unique perspective I offer here is in regard to (a) what happens to behaviors up and down the organization when terrible results are being posted and (b) how those who lead from the middle can positively influence the environment in such times.

More specifically, I've been conducting research for over two decades on how bad results change people's behavior, causing it to turn toxic at times, a result that cascades downward. This phenomenon can best be explained in what follows.

Think of the mass of water at the top of a waterfall, just before it plummets over the edge, turbulent and frothing (see Figure 6.3).

Figure 6.3 The Waterfall Effect

Source: Kristi Blokhin/Shutterstock.com

Now notice that bulk of water cascading downward with intense ferocity, each drop of water in a fast-moving freefall. Closer examination reveals that each drop of water impacts the path of the drop below it. It's immutable, such is the downward force of gravity. After the long descent into a frenzied gathering pool, the collective body of water races downstream, eventually settling into a smoother, less agitated rhythm.

Such is the flow of organizational behavior during times of bad results. It's when the Waterfall Effect can kick in, which says: just as every drop of water in a turbulent waterfall affects the course of other drops below it, so does every leader's behavior affect employees' behavior below him or her. Agitation begets agitation. It's just gravity. It's an unfortunate part of human nature. Eventually, things settle down further downstream, but not before the course of many individual behaviors has been altered.

Knowing that this is what happens in times of poor results helps you spot the cascade in action; the toxic behavior that hurls downward, from upper management, to you (trying to lead from the middle), to those down on the front line. Seeing it for what it is helps you to positively, not negatively, alter the path of others.

Here's what the toxic cascade might specifically look like. When things aren't going well, those at the top feel the turbidity the most, and it shows up as finger pointing, applying more pressure unnecessarily, losing patience more quickly more often, more micromanaging, more tenseness in every meeting, and forgetting to praise but always remembering to berate and belittle, among other undesirable outcomes. Such behavior can materially affect your outlook, attitude, and actions. It can cause you to unintentionally pass on the toxicity to those below you.

But in knowing this fundamental truth, you can defy gravity.

Remember that the poor behavior you're experiencing from those above you is just gravity, the weight of their toxic emotions and actions falling onto you, taking you off course. The leaders above you aren't always like this. They're likely good people at the core, but turmoil has changed them and as a result they interact differently with those below them, far more negatively than they normally would.

You can refuse to let your behaviors mirror those above you and negatively affect those below you. You can better forgive the behavior of those above you and choose to see it as just gravity; they're passing down what's been thrust upon them. And it's all starting from a chaotic source, the wildly churning waters from the stream that feeds into the waterfall (the bad results that have been building up).

While it may be coming fast and furious at you from above, you can avoid throwing the employees on your team into a frenzied, off-course misdirect with your words and actions. You can control the flow of actions and attitude from you on down and steer everyone into calmer, more reassuring waters.

This is another of the transformative, specialist elements of leading teams effectively from the middle. Let's cover one more.

Leading a Remote Team

A unique challenge for leaders in the middle is managing remote teams, something that was rapidly growing more common—until it became the only way forward for a while with the COVID-19 reality. Regardless of how you were introduced to leading remotely, here's how to do it well, based on research and experience: the 8 laws of effectively leading from a distance.

1. Remember that leading remotely is still leading

Just because you lead from afar doesn't mean all the leadership instincts you've been developing over the years are suddenly thrown out the window. Much of what feels right as a leader still applies; you're not starting over here. So, first, take a deep breath and ask yourself, WWLD—What Would Leaders Do? The actions might take a different form, but much of the intent remains.

2. Replicate the human need for face to face

We're a visual species. In fact, research from UCLA psychologist Albert Mehrabian shows an astonishing 55 percent of the feelings and attitudes others experience from what we communicate comes from our body language, with only 7 percent coming from the words we speak (and the other 38 percent coming from the tone of our voice).[2] So using video with remote employees, regularly, is an absolute requirement. Period.

By the way, resist the temptation to have your video feed framing only your face; instead, sit back far enough to include your upper body so body language and hand gestures can be seen as well.

3. Treat communication like a strategy, not an activity

Communication (or lack thereof) is the number-one barrier to effective manager/employee relationships in remote work. It's strategically vital to put exceptionally clear communication systems, processes, and agreements in place. Spend the amount of time and attention to detail on a communication plan that you would a key strategy—because that's what communicating effectively from a distance is, a strategy.

Establish a frequent video (and audio) meeting rhythm, one that allows for overcommunication while at the same time establishing clear boundaries—working remotely does not mean remotely having a life. And time zone differences or personal needs for flexibility triggered by working from a distance all must be baked into the plan as a basic cost of doing remote business.

4. Leading from a distance doesn't mean things have to feel distant

Remember that you're trying to replicate a culture and the human need for connection. In fact, every time you're on a video call, participants are reminded that, in fact, they aren't connected face to face in a physical sense. Thus, it's important to bring emotion and a feeling of connectedness into distanced communications. Help this along by investing in informal communication. For example, occasionally conduct a longer one-on-one to catch up on personal things or start video team meetings with chit-chat. In written communications, use gifs to connote the emotion you're trying to convey (emotion that's hard to fully transmit in an email or on an instant message). Pair up employees as "remote buddies" to encourage more frequent communication and to foster friendships.

And don't be distant about career discussions, either. Research shows that remote workers report having 25 percent fewer conversations about their career with their managers versus in-office employees.[3] So keep things personal, literally.

In general, it's important to recognize the biggest worries for remote workers, which all have to do with feeling left out. Research shows the specific biggest challenges are remote workers feeling isolated, worrying about "colleagues not fighting for my priorities," co-workers "making changes/decisions without looping me in," and concern about co-workers "lobbying against me/talking behind my back."[4] Let all of this serve as a reminder to close the emotional distance your remote workers feel.

5. Don't create second-class citizens

This is related to number 4 above but worthy of its own mention. It's regarding when you have a mixture of on-site and remote employees to lead. All too often, the out-of-sight remote employees become out-of-mind employees, who then effectively become second-class citizens.

It's helpful to mentally flip things. Think of the on-site employees, the ones who see you all the time and can drop by your office/cubicle whenever, as being second priority for communication responsiveness. Respond to remote employees immediately and be extra flexible in accommodating their need to meet. Ask on-site employees to be more intentional in scheduling times to connect with you. I'm not saying go overboard and now ignore on-site employees, I just mean for you to be disciplined about keeping everyone feeling equal.

6. Manage by objective, not observation

Forget "seeing is believing." While video is critical for managing remotely, that doesn't mean the point of you seeing employees is to confirm they're working. Focus on outcomes. Trust them and give them space. Focus on inquiries intended to help, not inquisitions intended to inspect. Use the face time to emotionally connect with them, set clear expectations, and to keep reinforcing the big picture, not as confirmation of effort. Leading from a distance requires your willingness to give the full benefit of the autonomy that naturally exists from the fact the employee is working remotely.

7. Leverage just as much technology as you need, and no more

Without question, getting the technology right to enable proper remote work is essential. Just approach the challenge with intention, not distraction. Have a plan for your group's remote communication needs and don't get caught in technology creep. Giving employees too many communication tools can cause confusion, burnout, and have the opposite effect of what you intended. In fact, one study showed an incredible 69 percent of employees waste an hour every day navigating between apps.[5]

Don't let that happen on your team. For example, perhaps you decide you need one application each for group chat, instant messaging, video meetings, email, screen sharing, and file sharing. And that's it. The point is to have a thoughtful plan to provide the technological tools employees need, without overcomplicating it.

8. Dial up your listening, asking, and flexibility skills

None of these will ever be more important than when working with remote employees.

So, run all the specialty plays in this chapter to run your team well from the middle. You'll amp up your influence all around. And speaking of all around, let's continue working across in the next chapter, which focuses on influencing peers.

Notes:

1. "Guide: Understand Team Effectiveness," rework.withgoogle.com.

2. A. Mehrabian, "Silent Messages—A Wealth of Information About Non-verbal Communication (Body Language)," kaaj.com.

3. "The State of Remote Work Report," owllabs.com.

4. "11 Essential Tips for Managing Remote Employees," getlighthouse.com.

5. "From Workplace Chaos to Zen," RingCentral, netstorage.ringcentral.com.

7 Influencing Peers

We turn our focus now to influencing peers, that is, co-workers important to achieving your goals but who aren't necessarily on a formal team you lead, and over whom you have no authority. Today's leader from the middle has more peers than ever to influence given the rise of matrixed organizations, which is tricky, as influencing peers is a nuanced practice. Not to fear, though, because in this chapter you'll get refined plays to help you be more effective in this aspect of leading across the organization.

Influencing peers effectively means starting with the right foundation and then building upon it by concentrating your efforts in four areas, or four pillars (Figure 7.1).

Let's first dig into the foundation and then build upwards from there.

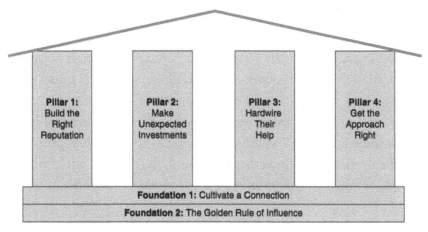

Figure 7.1 The Pillars of Peer Influence

Foundation 1: Cultivate a Connection

The truth is, more often than not peers are treated more like potential transactions than potential relationships. You can stand out among middle managers by simply making the effort to make a genuine connection with peers. Just like you would in any other relationship, take the time to get to know them and let them get to know you, and look for common beliefs, values, and experiences to build upon.

Building a connection with a peer also gives you the opportunity to play a unique role, different than in any other workplace relationship. You can be someone they can seek out to safely vent their frustrations, share their worries, commiserate, and in general, confide in. Your arm's-length distance is an advantage here; they don't report to you directly or indirectly as a team member (or vice versa), so they can be more open and see you as a much-needed outlet. Not only can this lead to a rewarding relationship, it puts the building blocks in place so that your peers know when you collaborate on something, your intent is pure.

Now, it can be difficult to put this connective foundation in place when dealing with a difficult peer. But I offer one powerful sentence that can change that. Before engaging with the problematic peer, remember this:

We all fear something, love something, have lost something.

Fear explains so much of undesirable human behavior. It engages our brain in the wrong conversation and distorts reality. It causes us to act in ways we don't intend or are unaware of. And the truth is, we all fear something. Even you. So, there's a decent chance that it's fear in some form that's making your difficult-to-work-with peer so difficult to work with. Perhaps they really fear failure, criticism, change, or rejection (yes, even rejection from you). Keep that in mind when trying to connect with this person. Ponder what the peer might fear, how it's affecting their behavior, and how you can better interact accordingly.

On the more positive side, we all love something, are loved by someone, and have the capacity to love. So even that miserable co-worker is loved by somebody, even if it's not you. And guess what? To be loved requires qualities worth loving. So, expand your own capacity to love and try to see those qualities in that difficult peer. See them for what they are that's wonderful to someone else rather than for what they aren't according to your narrower point of view.

Lastly, we most certainly have all lost something, including that difficult peer. It might literally be a loved one lost, even recently. Or perhaps your peer has lost their dignity, support, sense of confidence, or career momentum—all things that would have an understandable impact on one's behavior. Consider that and know that it's worth your compassion and patience when interacting with him or her.

Foundation 2: The Golden Rule of Influence

There has been plenty written on how to influence when you don't have any authority. Much that's shared in this book can be used to influence those whom you have no formal power over. But I believe the essence of doing so boils down to one basic directive, well-articulated by author Dan Schwartz. If you want to influence without leaning on your position power, think about people in your life who had no authority over you, yet were tremendously influential. Odds are, they had such an impact because they did it by doing four things: caring, listening, giving, and teaching (which we'll talk more about shortly).[1] That's it.

I think of this as the Golden Rule of Influence; influence others the same basic ways you were influenced. It's especially powerful for influencing peers you have no authority over because your willingness to care, listen, give, and teach isn't the norm and will be seen as true gifts. The absence of authority isn't a barrier to influencing because you're drawing on the basics of human emotion and empathy.

Pillar 1: Build the Right Reputation

You influence peers when you draw them to you, creating a desire for them to work more closely with you. That requires building a very specific reputation, one based on the fact that peers want to know two things about you.

First, can you be trusted? They don't work with you as often as they do others and they're already surrounded all day, every day, by people with hidden agendas.

Second, peers want to know if you're worth collaborating with to achieve a goal, that you're highly competent and credible and worth taking time away from those they work with more directly.

You build this very specific reputation when you become known for the following things.

1. Showing a willingness to help

Peers know you're not obligated to help but want to know you're genuinely willing to do so. This doesn't mean you have to be forever volunteering your services to every peer. Just being responsive to requests for help is an influential thing to be known for. In fact, one study showed that leaders who engaged in reactive helping (requests for help) drew more gratitude from the recipients than when they acted as a proactive helper.[2] Peers don't always fully appreciate you inserting yourself into their problem, however well-intended your offer of help is. Not that you can't be proactive in helping, it just requires more subtlety, like asking peers questions that will help them find the answers versus jumping in and outright solving their issue.

2. Exuding expertise in your area

Peers want to know that they can defer to you with confidence and that you've got your part of the mutual task well covered. You exude your expertise by always being well prepared for any meeting where you have to show leadership in your area of responsibility.

3. Being objective, logical, and data based

Your peers won't want to interact with overly emotional, uninformed decision-makers. If they're going to work with someone outside their chain of command, they'll want to know that their input and efforts will ultimately be a part of smart decisions made.

4. Representing your peers fairly, consistently keeping their point of view in mind, even when they're not present

Why would a peer want to help you or work more closely with you if you didn't?

5. Taking ownership of issues and never passing the buck, blaming, or backstabbing a peer

This goes straight to the core of trustworthiness. If peers are going to spend discretionary effort working with you, there's no room for you to do anything but consistently act in a trustworthy manner.

6. Shining in times of adversity

This is about being a beacon in dark times. Moments of adversity allow you to create impressionable moments, especially for those who might not see you in action every day.

7. Being sure to credit peers and give them honest praise and appreciation, never grabbing the glory

Your peers will also want to know their choice to engage more deeply with you will be a rewarding experience.

8. Exuding enthusiasm and a great attitude

It's hard not to be drawn to people who seem to love what they do. Especially since your peers likely already have to deal with plenty of negative nellies within their own reporting lines and teams.

9. Being vulnerable, admitting mistakes, and asking for advice

Peers have enough competition within their own silo of hierarchy and enough reason to feel as insecure as any other human being. So, they won't want to feel like they're interacting with a prima donna know-it-all when they don't have to.

To heighten your success and reputation in leading from the middle, make the effort to build a reputation for all the above. To build it, be it (consistently).

Pillar 2: Make Unexpected Investments

This goes beyond the Golden Rule of Influence (influencing others the same basic ways you're influenced). This is about going above and beyond to help your peers win and grow. If your peers indicate a willingness to receive this kind of investment from you, it's incredibly powerful because my experience shows that others outside their hierarchy will rarely make such an investment.

So, what do unexpected investments look like? The most powerful kinds come in two forms.

1. Peer-to-peer feedback

First, take the time to not just enlist and work with peers to achieve a goal, but to teach and mentor them along the way. Doing so includes helping them learn from thoughtful feedback, which can be highly effective as peer-to-peer feedback is the most objective kind.

But giving feedback to peers has one unique requirement. Harvard research indicates that peer-to-peer feedback doesn't work unless the recipient of the feedback feels truly valued by the giver of the feedback. In absence of feeling valued, the receiving peer will simply avoid giver peers and their feedback, instead seeking out more self-affirming co-workers. The researchers call this process "shopping for confirmation."[3] In other words, your peers may not want you shining a negative light on them (they get enough of that in their hierarchy); they'd much rather have you making them feel good about themselves. That is, unless they know you truly value them. Then your feedback is seen as you trying to give them a gift in the form of feedback.

To show you truly value peers, do the unexpected and compliment them on who they are, what they do, or how they do it. Be specific. Precision implies you care enough to notice and to take the time and brainpower to thoughtfully articulate your appreciation. As mentioned before, you can also seek out their feedback and advice (making it a two-way street), being sure to listen and act on it if appropriate.

2. Outright advocacy

The second major source of unexpected investment you can make in peers takes the form of outright advocacy. This is where you evangelize for what your peers are evaluated on, a potent way to show you're invested in their success. You do so by taking three specific steps.

Step 1: Find out what your colleagues get evaluated on. If they do a job similar to yours, you probably already know, but if they work in a different function, it's likely quite different. For example, your peer in R&D might get rewarded for being innovative, the co-worker who works in the plant gets measured on safety and efficiency of production, the person in finance on encouraging a balance of smart spending and cost cutting. If you don't know, ask people who work in that function what's important to demonstrate in that function.

Step 2: Find opportunities to share positive feedback on what matters to who matters. That is, share the praise with the co-worker's boss—praise on what matters and is measured as success in that peer's world.

Step 3: Let the peer know you're bragging on them to the boss. Do this from time to time. At other times, don't tell anyone—it tends to get back to the people anyway that you've been spreading positive gossip about them to their boss. This positive "blindside" is even more powerful than bcc'ing people on a praise email you wrote to their boss.

Making unexpected investments can lead to unexpectedly influential relationships with your peers. So, consider these two contributions of your time and effort.

Pillar 3: Hardwire Their Help

You seek to influence peers because you ultimately want their help on something in some form. The first two pillars involved indirect triggers; building the right reputation and making unexpected investments, both of which lead to eventual influence over time. But there are also mechanical methods to more immediately influence peers, ways to hardwire your influence by creating direct triggers. Here are the most effective ways.

1. Reciprocity

This is the cardinal rule of influencing peers. Do something for them and you ingratiate them—they'll feel compelled to do something for you. This doesn't mean be disingenuous and manipulative, giving something only so you'll get something. But it is human nature to reciprocate, and there's nothing wrong with using that to your influencing advantage.

And after doing something for them, you don't need to point out, even subtly, that now they owe you; they'll naturally feel a sense of obligation. It will be unspoken when you come to them for help; they'll remember your assistance and want to return the favor. After all, if you're doing it right, what you gave them helped them achieve a goal or avoid a negative, both things worthy of reciprocity.

2. Give them 10 percent more

This is a close cousin to reciprocity, but deserving of its own mention. If you always add value in your interactions with peers and visibly give that extra effort, they'll feel the need to bring their best, helping selves to the table as well when engaging with you. That's a form of direct influence.

3. Link your agenda to their agenda

Nothing gets people on the same page quicker than striving for common goals. So, don't think of your peers as a list of people you're trying to round up and corral to get your work done. Find out what their agenda is and make the connection to yours. Leveraging a common purpose, vision, mission, or goals are all great ways to do this.

4. Solve a problem together

It's one thing to help a peer or enroll their help. It's another to identify or get involved in a thorny mutual problem and tackle it with your
peer in partnership. The ups and downs of problem-solving will pull
you closer together, another direct form of influence.

Pillar 4: Get the Approach Right

Influencing peers requires knowing how to approach them in a way
that doesn't raise defenses, suspicions, or hackles. After all, you don't
have any hierarchical working relationship with them, so just what is it
you want from them anyway? Here's how to get the approach right so
you'll stick the landing.

1. Be clear on your context

Peers will know less than others about where you're coming from as
you approach them. So be transparent in your asks and offers.

2. Know what you're asking

Related to the above, be clear and direct in your asks and what will
be required from them. Don't downplay the size and scope of the
ask. Understand and acknowledge if what you need from them could
present problems in any way and offer ideas on how that "pain" can be
mitigated.

3. Know that they don't care about your deadlines

Also related to the above, all too often I've seen well-meaning middle
managers approach peers for help on something, impressing upon
them the urgency of the situation. Not ideal. Your emergency is not
their emergency. Instead, plan out when you might need to enroll

a peer on something and give them plenty of time and options for getting involved in the way you need them to.

4. Know your peers' job and motivations

I don't mean know everything about their role and all their heart's desires. Know enough about what their job entails, how your request intersects with that, and at least the basics of how they're rewarded. This allows you to have a more informed ask with more tangible, meaningful benefits to your peer that you can articulate upon your request. This is about encouraging the expenditure of their discretionary energy to aid your cause, so understanding where your peer is coming from is essential.

5. Let them have the ideas

As I alluded to in Chapter 5, what are you more motivated to work on, an idea that you came up with or one that was dictated to you by someone else? It's not even close. So, as you approach, engage, and ideate with peers, make them feel as if they came up with the ideas you want executed. Again, not in a disingenuous, manipulative way, but in a more deferring manner.

For example, ask questions that will elicit ideas, and when your peer shows excitement and desired ownership of one of those ideas, step back and defer to your peer, letting them run with the idea and continuing to shape it. Subtly refer to it as their idea and talk about the support you want to give to make their idea happen. (By the way, this tactic is not only effective across the organization with peers, but in leading up and down the organization too.)

6. Exert the opposite of peer pressure

I always thought peer pressure in the traditional sense was the wrong approach for any peer to use in an attempt to influence me. Getting me to do something because all my friends were doing it worked as a kid, and only works as an adult in more subtle, social influencer ways. As in, read this book because 657 people have given it five stars on amazon .com, and so forth. But peer pressure as a direct play in the workplace? Not so much. Your workplace peers won't succumb willingly and with good feelings about it just because you use old-school peer pressure. You already know this and likely wouldn't even consider it. But I find that leveraging the exact opposite approach to peer pressure is useful.

Here's what I mean. When enrolling peers for help, make a point that they won't need to adjust to you/your team's exact style and way of doing things. Instead, encourage the exact opposite. Invite them to bring their unique, individual self, skills, and style to the table. Make the opportunity to work with you feel like an opportunity for them to express their full selves in a safe environment, something they might not be feeling they can do in their current hierarchical structure.

So, by applying the specific tools in this chapter, you'll have peer power on your side. Let's continue turbocharging your ability to lead across the organization (and up and down as well) by focusing on a wildly important specialty skill, leading change, in the next chapter.

Notes:

1. D. Schwartz, "Be a Ground Floor Leader: Influence Your Peers," td.org (July 30, 2015).

2. H.W. Lee, J. Bradburn, R.E. Johnson, S. Lin, and C. Chang, "The Benefits of Receiving Gratitude for Helpers: A Daily Investigation of Proactive and Reactive Helping at Work," *Journal of Applied Psychology* 104, no. 2 (2019): 197–213.

3. S. Berinato, "Negative Feedback Rarely Leads to Improvement," *Harvard Business Review*, hbr.org (January 2018).

8 Leading Change

Nothing can catalyze, or paralyze, an organization quite like change. And while the middle, by definition, isn't at the end of anything, it's still the jumping-off point for change. Change simply won't happen without the mid-level players leading the way. It's middle managers who are closest to top brass who pass down change, who are in the best position to help them formulate change, who might create change themselves, and who are closest to those below who must live the (often emotionally charged) change. For change to flow down through an organization and stick, regardless of its source, it requires specialized know-how for those leading from the middle, especially since *over 70 percent* of change initiatives fail.

That's an astonishing number, often attributed to the fact that focus falls on just about anything other than the people who have to actually live the change. We'll be doing the opposite by focusing on change management, a disciplined approach for guiding individuals to successfully adapt to change and move to a better future state. In other words, it's managing the *human side* of change.

So let's dig in. You'll learn about the fundamental truths of leading change, you'll learn the related powerful change management model (EMC^2) that you can follow phase by phase, step by step, and you'll get specific plays for having one-on-one change conversations with employees to help them successfully adapt.

The Eight Truths of Leading Change

To lead change effectively first requires an understanding of the very nature of leading change. There are a set of fundamental truths you'll experience as you navigate this tricky responsibility, truths that inform the change management approach that follows in the next section. So, let's first dive into truth.

1. Change elicits an emotional journey

Leading change effectively first requires understanding how people process change and why it's so difficult for so many. It starts with our wiring. We're wired for survival; it's been that way dating back to cavepeople times. Change threatens our survival instinct. And while change itself is unpredictable, our reaction to it isn't. In fact, in the 1960s, psychiatrist Elisabeth Kübler-Ross identified what's known as the Change Curve. Modeled after her original work on the stages of grief, it's what every human being goes through when facing change. I've taken Kübler-Ross's work and others' interpretation of it and blended it with my own work in change management to share the perspective illustrated in Figure 8.1.

Let's walk through the curve from left to right. When change happens, by default the **status quo** is shaken. There's often indignation

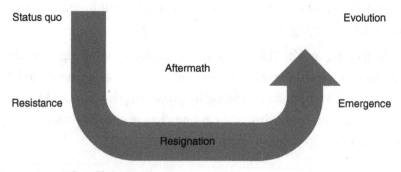

Figure 8.1 The Change Curve

and even shock: "How could they do this?," "How could this happen to me?" A surge of energy goes into denying that the change is happening which can quickly blend into a prolonged **resistance** phase laced with anger, finger pointing, dejection, and getting stuck at "It's not fair."

This leads into the **resignation** phase where it's accepted that the change is indeed happening, and where energy and morale drops to its lowest point. It's vital that the individual's journey through the curve, especially up to this point, is supported with empathy, active listening, and well-thought-through support mechanisms (all of which the model that follows incorporates).

Eventually, people enter the **emergence** stage, emerging from their funk to productively engage in the change, exploring ways they can move forward and the possibilities the change holds.

This leads into the first signs of **evolving**, where behaviors change and the individual integrates new approaches into his or her way of being.

In the **aftermath** stage, people reflect, often realizing the change wasn't so bad after all and that they've even grown from it. At some point, the status quo is interrupted once again and the curve starts all over.

Of course, we all go through the curve at different speeds and intensity levels. I know people who love change; when the status quo is shaken they zip instantly to evolving and adapting accordingly. That's not most of us, however. It's also important to note that you can go back and forth on the curve. For example, you can find yourself in the emergence stage, only to encounter something about the change that pulls you back into resistance mode.

Knowing all this, you can let employees know that they're not alone in what they're feeling; everyone goes through this curve in their own way. And raising everyone's awareness of this very human curve helps usher everyone to the positive aftermath much more quickly.

2. Successful change is more than a process, it's a path

If you're leading change properly, employees will see it as a path to a better way forward, not merely a process to endure. Change will be seen not as a series of painful moments to labor through but as pivotal moments in which to think big and use as a jumping off point to change one's trajectory—professionally and personally.

3. It's not the change itself that's painful, it's the transition

People don't actually hate the change itself as much as you think. It's the painful transition from the old way to the new way that they dislike (as the Change Curve indicates). This means that change leaders must have a plan not just for changing processes or systems, but also for helping people make the transition. A client of mine appoints a "Chief Change Officer" to every change initiative. The CCO's job is to (and this is straight from the job description) "help people thrive, not just survive, in change." That spirit is right on.

So, this means that as the leader of change you have to sweat the details of transition. We'll lay those details out throughout this chapter.

4. Go slow to go fast

Most leaders want to rush change. (This was one of my issues as a younger mid-level leader.) After all, no change ever initiated didn't have a ton of associated work with it; you naturally want to progress things, quickly. Even if you have a fast approaching date by which the change must be implemented, you still have to plan for and act as if the change will take time to seep in, because it will. Slowing things down in this way will actually allow you to speed up the implementation of change over the long run. As we progress through this chapter, you'll understand what takes time and where your time should be spent to successfully implement change.

5. Change is historical

Meaning, change always happens within the context of an individual's past experience with change. Each individual can't help but view change through that lens. You'll see this come into play in both the change management model and the one-on-one change conversation guide that follows.

6. Change is really about changing habits

Psychology and marketing teach us that there's nothing more difficult than trying to change a habit. So, you have to keep in mind not only the truths of leading change, but the rules of habit change, which we'll cover in the EMC^2 model.

7. Successful change requires visible champions

If employees don't see their leaders, especially their leaders in the middle, walking the talk and demonstrating the importance of change (spoiler alert), it comes across as unimportant. Change is hard enough to ingrain in employees; if they don't have visible role models and reinforcements, it has no chance to stick.

8. Effective change happens sequentially

By this I don't mean that change itself literally happens in a very predictable, step-by-step fashion. Change bounces us all around, out of order, all the time. What I mean is that effectively leading and managing change requires an overall disciplined, sequential, approach. And while I indicated in the second truth that change is more than a process (i.e., it shouldn't feel like one), it still needs some process to be implemented effectively. In fact, the change management process requires three very specific phases (and one "pre-phase"), which we'll move to next.

The EMC^2 Change Model

Welcome to a proven change management model that incorporates the best of other existing change models while building on the back of the 8 truths of leading change, all wrapped into a tidy acronym, EMC^2. The acronym plays on Albert Einstein's formula e=mc^2, which is the formula for energy (energy = mass x the speed of light squared). With that in mind, think of this as the model for *getting mass energy behind change*, which is exactly what's required if you want to succeed in leading change, especially from the middle.

The acronym also stands for the sequential phases that mid-level leaders must spearhead to yield effective, energizing change. Note that the actions taken in each phase can overlap, the phases are more about providing "law and order" to the change management process. Also note that before you even get to Phases 1–3 (which derive the EMC^2 acronym), some groundwork is required in Phase 0. Here's what each of these phases are, then we'll go into detail on each one.

Phase 0: Conduct a Change Readiness Assessment

Phase 1: Evoke enthusiasm for change

Phase 2: Move employees to commitment

Phase 3: Create new habits^2 (the squared denotes the doubling of effort needed at this stage)

Phase 0: Conduct a Change Readiness Assessment

This is about having your ducks in a row (as the saying goes) before you fully engage your organization in the implementation of change. If you aren't disciplined in assessing your own readiness, that of others leading the change with you, and that of the recipients of the change, how can you expect to beat the odds in executing a truly successful program of change? Focus on the four concise steps that follow to make sure you're ready to go.

Specific steps:

1. Get clear on exactly what's changing and why. This boils down to asking yourself (and fellow change leaders) the following half-dozen questions—and continually re-asking them if necessary until you're satisfied with the answers:

- *Are you clear on what problem you're solving with the change, and is it the right problem (i.e., the real underlying issue)?*
- *Are you avoiding "change drift" (when more changes are instituted than necessary or the changes don't really address the issue you intend)?*
- *Do you understand, in detail, what policies, processes, and systems must change and why? Which jobs are impacted in what way?*
- *Do you have a clear vision for the change—what will ultimately be accomplished and what it will look like to the organization?*
- *Do you know who the key owners of the change are?*
- *Do you know how you'll measure if the change is successful or not?*

2. Assess the skill, the will, and the hill. This next step is about understanding the organization's readiness and capacity for change. It involves assessing the current state of the organization on three fronts and comparing to what's needed in light of the change coming. Plans should then be made to fill any gaps between where the organization is and what's needed.

Specifically, consider the skill, will, and hill, meaning, ask these specific questions:

- *What's the **skill** level of the organization and what new knowledge, skills, and training will employees need to develop to thrive in the desired future state?*

- *What's the **will** of the organization for facing change? What are the current behaviors and attitudes and what adjustments will be required? Is the organization ready to take on the added work of implementing the change? What work can be eliminated or reprioritized to accommodate?*

- *What's the **hill** the organization faces in successfully implementing the change? What are the barriers to overcome?*

Just thinking to ask these questions is half the battle. The other half is to then put plans in place to upskill the employees as needed, to have a plan for influencing behaviors and attitudes, to take into account current workloads and find opportunities to eliminate work to accommodate new work, and to eliminate as many barriers as possible up front and have a response plan when other expected barriers materialize. The detail in Phases 1–3 in the EMC^2 model will help you with all of this.

3. Get meaningful early input from stakeholders.   No change should be executed in a vacuum, devoid of input from those whom the change will affect most. Make sure you've gotten early input on the change itself and the implementation plan; it's an easy step to skip. As mentioned previously, change leaders can rush this, bypassing the opportunity to gather insights and reality checks, all of which could have been incorporated into the plan.

Even better if you can break the change into pieces and test some of the pieces before going "live" with it. I know of a company that bought tens of millions of dollars of new assembly line equipment for their manufacturing plants—a huge change to dramatically different machines. They picked one of their smallest facilities and tested each phase thoroughly: installation, operation, and maintenance. They enrolled those on the line working with the new equipment and regularly sought their input— thus working out a ton of bugs that allowed a smooth migration to the new equipment in all the remaining plants.

4. Establish a Change Coalition.   This is a team of key leaders, starting with you, who serve as visible, role-model change champions. These should be people who are enthusiastic about the change, but not blindly so. In other words, they're people who acknowledge the limitations and challenges of implementing the change and see it through the eyes of employees living the change. The coalition should leverage a message track when addressing the organization about change. This ensures consistency of communication, which is vital for employees to accept and move forward with change. Multiple methods of communication should also be established. For example, town hall meetings, employee bulletins, email, or one-on-one change conversations—which we'll get into in a bit.

The coalition can also include "employee change champions," enthusiastic early adopters of the change who can help spread positive messaging.

Now, with everything in order after conducting your Change Readiness Assessment, you can engage in the EMC^2 model (Phases 1–3), which will guide you on how to engage your organization in the change ahead.

Phase 1: Evoke enthusiasm for change

General change management theory speaks to the importance of creating awareness for and acceptance of the need for change (which you've already started building after conducting a Change Readiness Assessment in Phase 0). But this model raises the bar, going beyond awareness and acceptance to creating *enthusiasm* for change. It's necessary—recall the 70 percent failure rate of change initiatives. It might feel like a lot to ask given so many feel the opposite of enthusiasm for change, but with the right proven steps, you'll succeed. Let's take it one step at a time.

Specific steps:

1. Transparently express the state of the union and compare it to a desirable future.   Describe to your audience where the organization is today and compare it to where the change will take the organization. It should be a clear, simple, yet compelling vision, including specifically what's changing, why, by when, and how it links to the organization's broader purpose, goals, and strategies. It's this comparison that makes the change feel like a conduit to a better, compelling future state, like an exciting path versus a deplorable process. And make clear what *won't* change—it's these elements of stability that anchor employees and that help them through the difficult aspects of change.

Unfortunately, change leaders can unintentionally dampen enthusiasm (versus the opposite) at this point, in several ways.

First, by jumping right to sharing the change vision (the desired endpoint) while neglecting to draw a contrast to the current state of the union and explaining why status quo is unacceptable (i.e., the danger of *not* changing). By not drawing the contrast, it's a missed opportunity; the bigger the contrast, the more excitement generated, and the stronger the case for change. Which brings us to the next, related misstep.

And that is, the vision doesn't feel purposeful, exciting, or attainable, and/or the underlying supporting reasons for change are simply unconvincing. This is a killer issue that must be addressed with careful framing, messaging, and reworking until the vision sings and the case for change is airtight.

Finally, even when describing the state of the union, many leaders fail to do so respectfully. They unintentionally (or intentionally) bash the past and alienate those in the audience who might have played a role in the current state of affairs. You need everyone enthused moving forward.

Any of these mistakes can prevent employees from understanding or accepting the change, let alone being enthused about it.

One other challenging scenario worth mentioning here: when you've been handed a change to implement that you don't agree with or that personally affects you in a negative way. While it's difficult and unfair, you simply must get yourself to a place of acceptance and understanding so you can exude a sense of comfort, confidence, and inspiration when talking the change with employees.

2. Articulate the impact the change will personally have on employees. Clearly articulate "what's in it" for the employees in the short and long term, tying it to professional and personal benefit. And be clear about the short and long-term negative impacts, too. The honesty will be appreciated and will give you more credibility when you're touting the benefits.

For those anticipating negative effects, show empathy and respect (remember the Change Curve). Acknowledge what's being left behind, even while you're gently reinforcing how much is being gained.

A great place to discuss the personal impacts of change with employees is during a one-on-one change conversation, which we'll get to shortly.

3. Create excited urgency. There's urgency, and then there's excited urgency. Urgency encourages action based on a fear of repercussions. Excited urgency inspires action based on excitement for the end-state. There's nothing wrong with the former; it's critical, in fact, for change to succeed. But this is about creating enthusiasm, so foster the latter, too.

You do so by continually communicating the benefits of the change. Share stories of successful past change and how it was grounded in necessity. Break the change into pieces and offer tangible rewards and celebration along the way to create anticipation for hitting the next milestone. A client of mine broke a huge change initiative into distinct phases and developed an "Excitement Escalation" plan, whereby the completion of each phase triggered increasingly larger rewards for employees. It started with iPod and iPad giveaways and worked its way up to surprise salary increases for everyone. Sign me up for that!

Barriers to overcome:

Because change is so difficult for so many people, barriers to successfully implementing it will arise, often dooming the effort to failure. But not for you, because what follows identifies the most common barriers when trying to create enthusiasm for change, and how to overcome them. Account for these in your change resistance plan.

1. Contestability or skepticism of the reasons for change. As

mentioned earlier, if your reasons for change aren't convincing, or if employees don't see the personal benefit to changing, good luck. The solve here is to keep working how you frame the reasons for and the benefits to change until they feel truly compelling from the employee's point of view, not just from your point of view.

Apple excels at generating excitement when they make a change or upgrade a product. They clearly illuminate the need for the change and make it feel like the consumer won't be able to live without the benefits. They even do so with fanfare and flare in their on-campus theater, leaving little room for skepticism.

2. Under-communicating the change vision by 10 times. A former CEO of Procter & Gamble once told me that your change vision has to be communicated 10 times more than the ordinary directive. All those times you don't communicate the vision represent missed opportunities to inspire. As mentioned previously, be sure to have a clear change message track or talking points for you and your key "change officers," and keep hammering them home, over and over. Under communicating can only be solved by, you guessed it, overcommunicating. So do it.

3. Misinformation, rumors, uncertainty, fear. Clarity, frequency, and honesty in communication will go a long way toward quashing all of this, as will keeping the emotional journey in mind that employees are going through (per the Change Curve). And know that employees often have a perception that they'll lose power in some way due to change. Be clear where this is actually the case, but reassure where it's not, reinforcing the value each employee brings to the table (and thus the power they still have).

You can also share the OAR acronym detailed in Chapter 3 with employees to help them overcome their distaste for uncertainty. Finally, encourage employees to think of change like a personal software upgrade; if they "download" the change, they'll get to You 2.0 (an even better version of themselves).

4. Structures or systems that fight the change. Employees' eagerness to migrate to a new state is severely dampened when things supporting the old state are still readily available. It makes it easier to disengage in the new way and in general harder to move on. That's especially true of old structures, systems, or processes still available that are counterintuitive to the change being implemented. Such things simply must go. For example, I know a company (let's call it "Dawdle Inc.") that spent millions on a hi-tech videoconferencing system, only to discover that employees were quietly still using the old teleconferencing system out of habit. IT got involved and made the old system unavailable while adding staff to train employees on the new system. Enthusiasm for the new way was instantly reignited.

Phase 2: Move employees to commitment

With a base of enthusiasm generated, it's time to migrate employees to feeling personally invested in the change and committed to seeing it through. Even when employees are enthused about change, it can take prodding to get them off the sidelines, to stop begrudgingly letting change happen *to* them versus getting fully engaged to make change happen *for* them. Here's how to get employees from excited to committed, from interested to invested.

Specific steps:

1. Feed the know-how. At this point, employees should understand why change is needed and what needs to change. Now they'll want to know *how* to change—what they need to do as they move from the old state to the new state, what's expected of them, and how to excel at their jobs in the new state. It's hard for employees to feel invested if they feel hopelessly "behind the curve" in terms of what knowledge they must acquire to successfully adapt. The good news is you've already done the groundwork to address this given the Change Readiness Assessment you conducted in Phase 0. Now it's time to put your best foot forward by sharing the BEST Guide with employees, a document that spells out the following:

Behaviors—what are the specific behaviors employees need to exhibit and actions they need to take as they transition and adapt?

Expectations—what are the overall expectations of employees as they transition and adapt?

Skills—what are the specific skills and knowledge employees need to develop as they transition and adapt?

    <u>T</u>raining—what support can the employees expect? What training, coaching, supporting processes, and resources will be provided?

    Sharing this document provides clarity on expectations, helps with the "how," and shows your commitment to supporting employees (while "forcing" you to articulate exactly how). Seeing your commitment helps them commit.

    Especially important here is to not underestimate the gap between current knowledge and abilities and what's needed in the new state. An accurate assessment ensures that the skills you're asking employees to develop and the training you're committing to provide truly sets them up for success. Put extra emphasis on pinpointing the skills required and training to be provided for those whose jobs will change the most.

2. Leverage the "Circles of Commitment"   Commitment to change further solidifies when you leverage three overlapping dynamics, helping employees feel three things in particular, as shown in Figure 8.2.

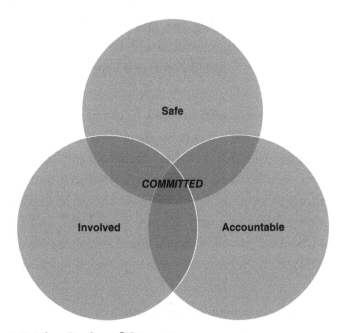

Figure 8.2 The Circles of Commitment

As Figure 8.2 illustrates, when employees feel safe, involved, and accountable, it takes them beyond enthusiasm to commitment.

Feeling **safe** means operating in a psychologically safe environment (touched upon in Chapter 6, "Leading Teams"). You provide this when you assure employees they have the competence for change and that they'll be supported throughout the journey, even as they make mistakes.

The support can take many forms. For example, offer empathetic words, share stories of your own change experiences, have patience for the learning process and tolerance for mistakes, and give employees easy access to the training and supporting resources they need. Just as important is to give employees the opportunity to practice new skills, replacing judgment with coaching. The point here is that change is daunting enough—employees need to feel supported, not exposed.

Feeling **involved** means employees have a place to voice their concerns, feel heard, and have a hand in shaping how change is implemented. Ask them to share their emotions, experiences, insights, and ideas. Big changes are a big deal, and employees need help to process it and a forum to get involved with it. The less they become involved, the more they'll feel like change is happening to them rather than for them.

There are many ways to do this well, it just takes a little creativity. For example, I keynoted for a client at their "Change Forward Conference," a two-day offsite that served as a forum for employees to learn about a major organizational change being introduced, and that gave the opportunity to input on details of how it should be implemented. Another client of mine conducts "Change Town Halls" and established a "Change Channel," an online forum where employees can post concerns and ideas, with a response from change leaders guaranteed within 24 hours.

By the way, don't forget to act on as much of the input as feasible. Doing so not only strengthens employee commitment to the change, it helps employees feel a sense of control—something compromised during change.

Feeling **accountable** comes from employees understanding their roles and responsibilities associated with change, knowing what needs to change by when in what way, understanding expectations and consequences if expectations aren't met, and recognizing how they're being measured. Tactfully reinforce all of this along the way as appropriate, with a supportive tone, using the BEST Guide as a place to start. Doing so is sure to further encourage employee commitment. Many times as a change leader, I was held accountable for holding employees accountable for implementing change. In each case, the accountability at every level helped the change initiative succeed.

It's important to note that all of these dynamics overlap and work in concert with one another, so it's vital to foster all three. For example, if employees feel safe, they're more likely to get involved, and won't feel threatened by being held accountable. Likewise, if they're involved, it decreases uncertainty and adds to their sense of feeling safe, which means they won't feel threatened by accountability. Finally, if employees feel accountable, they'll want to get involved to control more of their destiny, and will yearn to feel safe as they strive to achieve what they're being held accountable for. You get the idea.

3. Create commitment in context. The extent to which people commit and adapt to change (or not) has much to do with their personal context, their past personal experiences with change. Bad experiences create skepticism toward future change initiatives and a resistance to personally invest again. You'll have a hard time moving any employee forward without understanding what their experiences are and how their personal context raises barriers for adapting to the change at hand. Without knowing how they view past change, you can't discuss how this change effort will be different or could be tailored to avoid history repeating itself.

You discover all of this by having one-on-one change conversations with your employees. (See the "One-on-One Change Conversation Guide" at the end of this chapter.)

Barriers to overcome:

As in the first phase, there are several common barriers to anticipate and work through. In the case of this phase, what follows are the barriers to getting employees fully invested in making the change happen.

1. Change fatigue.   Constant change can leave employees exhausted at the mere thought of having to invest in yet another change. Acknowledge their fatigue and keep sharing the vision of why the change is happening. Keep reinforcing the importance of the change and the associated personal benefits. Eliminate as much "busy work" that comes with change as you can, like filling out forms or other administrative distractions.

Employees can also get burned out trying to adapt to too much change all at once. In your understandable eagerness to get to the change-induced state, it's easy to overload employees and try to do too much, too fast. Resist this temptation and carefully consider your employees' capacity to change. And remember, it's okay to go slow to go fast. Give time for employees to learn new skills or for needed processes or systems to be put into place. I'm not saying don't be aggressive and have a sense of urgency in implementing the change, just be realistic and plan for the time it will take to execute it well.

2. Lack of change champions, presence of change blockers.   By this stage of the game, employees will have a hard time committing to change if they don't see their leaders committed. They need to see visible change champions higher in the organization role-modeling the way, especially since it should now be clear how much work is involved in adapting.

On the other side of the coin, witnessing change blockers certainly won't help, either. By change blockers I mean key managers, who instead of helping lead change, openly *resist* it, even doing workarounds. While an absence of visible change champions disheartens employees, change blockers outright confuse them. They cause doubt that the change is important or that it will ever really be implemented.

Regarding a lack of visible change champions, the solve here goes back to the need to create a Change Coalition, as discussed earlier. Recall that it's also very effective to enroll employees committed to the change to serve as change agents. Give these employees specific tasks that allow them to voice their support for the change, to role-model desired behaviors, and to encourage "peer-to-peer commitment."

Regarding change blockers, calling them out takes courage but is a must. Don't make it about them as a person, but about the impact their visible resistance to change is having on the organization. Altering their behavior will make a big difference. To illustrate, I remember an organizational restructuring where a department responsible for innovation was downsized and much of their work redistributed elsewhere. A key manager in that department kept acting, quietly, as if nothing had changed, causing great confusion and shattering others' commitment to migrate to the new structure. It wasn't until that manager's unacceptable behavior was directly addressed by a peer that the new structure came to fruition (and became a big success).

3. Capacity scarcity. Change doesn't happen in a vacuum, employees still have to do their "day job" while transitioning and adapting to the new state. That takes time and effort, neither of which employees will feel like they have the capacity for. It's as common as it is understandable.

The Change Readiness Assessment you conducted will help as you'll have already identified work you can eliminate or reprioritize to accommodate new work required. Now is the time to make that real. Employees should actually see some form of their current work being eliminated or simplified. Perhaps it's a dose of bureaucratic work they no longer have to do, reports they no longer have to provide, or some drastically simplified process or system. The point is to make it substantive, not just symbolic.

At the same time, help employees move quickly through "in-betweenity," where they're stressed about letting go of the old ways but not yet adept at the new ways. Do this by making the old ways unavailable sooner and by providing training, coaching, and access to experts to help them become adept at the new ways faster (recall the "Dawdle Inc." example).

Finally, allow employees time to do the transition and adaptation work, so everything doesn't feel additive.

On to the final phase in the EMC^2 model.

Phase 3: Create new habits[2]

In the end, employees successfully adapt to change when they change habits. If you don't change *ongoing* behaviors and actions, you really haven't changed anything.

But changing habits is hard. I learned from spending many years as a leader in marketing just how difficult it is to get consumers to change their habits. Want someone to change from sweeping floors or using a mop to instead using a Swiffer? Sounds great, but it requires many years and hundreds of millions of dollars in marketing and advertising to convince consumers to switch. Want consumers to develop a new habit of spraying a room with Febreze to keep the air smelling fresh? No less effort. You get the idea. You won't create new habits for anyone to do anything without being very intentional about the effort you put into it. Implementing change in an organization is no different, and it takes twice as much effort as you might think to change habits (hence the ^{2} in EMC^2). Not to worry, though—put energy into these steps to make change stick.

Specific steps:

1. Follow the laws of habit change. If you want employees to form new habits, it's critical that the desired new behaviors and supporting new systems and processes meet four conditions.[1] They should be:

- obvious
- attractive
- easy to implement
- satisfying

For example, say you're responsible for improving team communication while at the same time have been charged with dramatically reducing the use of email. You have many communication applications to choose from to help with this, like Slack, Microsoft Teams, Google Hangouts, etc. As you're evaluating options, it dawns on you that this is about creating a new habit. That means, whatever platform you pick should be integrated into everyday use (thus obvious), should have many benefits to using (thus is attractive), should be easy to implement, and should be satisfying, perhaps due to a user-friendly interface.

At the same time, to help employees break old habits so they can concentrate on forming new ones, the behaviors, systems, and processes associated with the "old way" should meet four opposite conditions. They should be:

- invisible
- unattractive
- difficult
- unsatisfying

Continuing with our example, the email platform then should be much harder to access (thus "invisible"), unattractive to use (perhaps some of the email archiving features are stripped away), difficult to implement (email runs slower now), and should be unsatisfying (again, perhaps because some features are gone).

The point is, it takes discipline to enable the old saying, "Out with the old, in with the new."

2. Help develop new routines.   When employees have new routines to follow, they form new, familiar patterns, which lead to new habits. If a new routine is called for, help employees design it. For example, a client of mine made major changes to how they wanted their salespeople to call on new prospects each day. They created "Routine Maps" for each salesperson, documents mapping out ideal prospecting routines, including small steps and specific actions to take and micro-goals to achieve. They gave employees a chance to practice their new routines in a psychologically safe environment and reinforced validity of the routines by celebrating wins along the way.

It worked. And helping to develop new routines for your employees can work, too.

3. Keep revisiting what's at stake.   People are more likely to build a habit of exercise not just by faithfully repeating their exercise routines, but also by reminding themselves *why* they're exercising (to lose weight, look better, to combat a disease state, etc.). It's no different with forming habits in the face of change. Keep revisiting why the change is happening and what's at stake. Use the multiple communication channels you've already established to do so. Leverage the measurement systems you've put in place to let employees know exactly how they're doing along the way in implementing the change. Remember to create a mixture of urgency and excited urgency.

Barriers to overcome:

In forging new habits and working to make change stick, any of the barriers in prior phases can get in the way, so a holistic change resistance plan is required. On top of that, there's one more barrier to be mindful of in this final phase.

Entrenchment. In the face of substantive changes, the leader of change will face pockets of resistance, workarounds, and employees going back to old ways and habits. Fortitude is required here as is a commitment to remain a champion of the change. This includes tirelessly communicating what the change is ultimately meant to accomplish. It's also important to remember that you get the behavior you tolerate, so be firm about holding employees accountable. In the end, even though employees might not like change, change they must.

The One-on-One Change Conversation Guide

As I've mentioned, every person's experience with change is shaped by their past experiences with it. These experiences can form biases, fears, assumptions, and perceptions that can negatively affect the individual's ability to embrace and flourish in future change. So, understand and address this reality head-on. The best way to do so is to conduct one-on-one change conversations—leader-initiated, empathy-driven discussions between boss and each individual employee (or at least employees who appear to be struggling with the change). This is a time to have the Change Curve very much top of mind and to understand where the employee is on the curve.

In having these conversations, the idea is to give employees the chance to voice their concerns, share emotions, experiences, insights, and ideas. This also allows you to understand what LinkedIn VP Mike Derezin calls the "support continuum."[2] Regarding the change, is the employee:

- a passive resistor? (they quietly oppose it)
- an active resistor? (they openly oppose it)
- neutral to it?
- a passive supporter? (they quietly support it)
- an active supporter? (they openly support it)

Asking employees where they are on the spectrum enables good discussion and helps you understand where they're at with the change. To help them become active supporters, actively listen, show empathy, and help them overcome individual barriers that surface. Help employees articulate how the change could lead to professional and personal benefit. Help them get unstuck from their old narrative to write a new story.

It can also be powerful to let employees know that the ability to adapt effectively to change is critical for their development and progression. I surveyed 1,000 top executives around the globe, asking them what the leading indicator of a high-potential employee was—that is, the most important signal that someone should be moved upward quickly in their organization. "Ability to thrive in change" consistently ranked number one, above having a continuous improvement mindset, the ability to influence upward, having a mix of visionary and executional skills, and decisiveness.

Here's a time-tested set of a dozen prompts to enable this important one-on-one discussion. Ask employees these specific questions to understand what's getting in the way of (or what would help) the successful adoption of the change being implemented.

- *"Obviously, we're going through a lot of change. How are you feeling about it? What questions does it create?"*

- *"Change often causes us to give up or lose something. What do you fear giving up or losing?*

- *"What about this change leaves you feeling uncertain/worried?"*

- *"What part of this change is creating an obstacle for you?"*

- *"Do you anticipate unintended consequences as a result of this change?"*

- *"What's been your experience with other changes you've been through?"*

- *"How might you benefit from this change? What part of the change presents the greatest opportunity for you?"*

- *"Do you understand your role in this change?"*

- *"Do you understand what's expected of you with this change?"*

- *"How committed are you to making this change work, on a scale from 1 to 10?"* (or use the support continuum described previously)

- *"What resources or assistance do you need to make this change work?"*

- *"Any thoughts on how this change might best be implemented or things to watch out for?"*

As you ask these questions, of course, it's vital that you listen to the responses with empathy.

Up to a point, that is.

As a leader in the middle with so many constituents of change to worry about all around you, you can only show so much empathy in any given change conversation. At some point, the employee will simply have to accept that change is happening and that they can be part of a problem or part of a successful implementation. I recommend that each change conversation proceed with cascading levels of empathy as shown in Figure 8.3.

In reference to Figure 8.3, start at the top where you **listen** and empathize, share your own experiences with change, discuss barriers

Listen	Listen, listen, listen. Empathize, empathize, empathize. Relate your own painful experiences with change.	*Green*
Overcome	Help them overcome any barriers and concerns that surface. Reassure them that they have the competence to flourish.	*Green*
Reinforce	Reinforce the state of the union, why change is needed (including the danger of not changing) and the vision for the change. Close with expectation setting.	*Yellow*
Lay Down the Law	Restate the specific responsibilities and behaviors associated with the change that are expected. Make the natural consequences of not meeting those expectations clear.	*Red*

Figure 8.3 The Degrees of Empathy Scale

that arise, and encourage employees that they have the competence to **overcome** and flourish. This initial phase is color-coded green to encourage you to dive right in with confidence; every one-on-one change conversation can benefit from this starting point.

Depending on how the conversation is going, you might not need to **reinforce** much of anything (the next phase). If you're still sensing resistance, though, proceed with caution (thus it's color-coded yellow), meaning, continue showing empathy but don't back down as you reinforce all the points listed at this level in Figure 8.3. Overall here, be objective and firm.

Finally, if resistance to change continues to come up in the conversation, you may need to proceed all the way down to a lower empathy point where you **lay down the law**, restating responsibilities and behaviors required, and discussing consequences of not adapting. It's coded red as a reminder that it's time to draw a halt to further discussion—it's the tough love portion to draw on if needed.

Now it's time to put all the tools from this book into one toolbox and help you customize a set that's right for you, which we'll do in the final chapter.

Notes:

1. J. Clear, "Atomic Habits," Penguin Random House, p. 54, (2018).

2. M. Derezin, "Leading Your Team Through Change," linkedin.com/learning (April 24, 2019).

9 Creating Your Personal MAP (Middle Action Plan)

T his book is a playbook, jam-packed with plays to help you exude influence from the middle. No one would expect you to run every play, to absorb every piece of advice, to use every single tool in this book. That said, Figure 9.1 will help you easily remember all of the tools available to you in this book (at a high-level).

That's the overview. Now, if desired, you can get into more detail and build a customized plan that's tailored to your interests and needs, to meet you where you're at. Using the template in Figure 9.2, build your own personal MAP (Middle Action Plan) by selecting the tools/plays that are right for you in your current situation, by spending time revisiting and fully absorbing those tools, and then by diligently listing out the associated specific actions that you'll take.

The success of any organization goes as those who lead from the middle go. There's no job in any organization more critical, challenging, or exhilarating when done well. To do so requires understanding

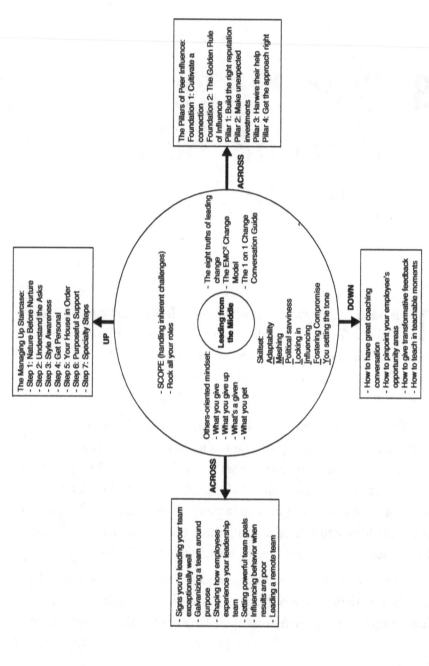

The Managing Up Staircase:
- Step 1: Nature Before Nurture
- Step 2: Understand the Asks
- Step 3: Style Awareness
- Step 4: Get Personal
- Step 5: Your House in Order
- Step 6: Purposeful Support
- Step 7: Specialty Steps

UP

The Pillars of Peer Influence:
Foundation 1: Cultivate a connection
Foundation 2: The Golden Rule of Influence
Pillar 1: Build the right reputation
Pillar 2: Make unexpected investments
Pillar 3: Hardwire their help
Pillar 4: Get the approach right

ACROSS

- SCOPE (handling inherent challenges)
- Rock all your roles

- The eight truths of leading change
- The EMC² Change Model
- The 1 on 1 Change Conversation Guide

Leading from the Middle

Others-oriented mindset:
- What you give
- What you give up
- What's a given
- What you get

Skillset:
Adaptability
Meshing
Political savviness
Locking in
Influencing
Fostering Compromise
You setting the tone

DOWN

- How to have great coaching conversation
- How to pinpoint your employee's opportunity areas
- How to give transformative feedback
- How to teach in teachable moments

ACROSS

- Signs you're leading your team exceptionally well
- Galvanizing a team around purpose
- Shaping how employees experience your leadership team
- Setting powerful team goals
- Influencing behavior when results are poor
- Leading a remote team

Figure 9.1 Quick Reference Guide of Tools in this Book

Tools available in this book	Tools I need right now	Specific actions I'll take
Handling challenges inherent in leading from the middle		
• SCOPE—A reframework to reshape the way you see, experience, react to, and resolve <u>S</u>elf-Identity, <u>C</u>onflict, <u>O</u>mnipotence, <u>P</u>hysical, and <u>E</u>motional challenges inherent in leading from the middle (see chapter 1 for plenty of reorienting insights).		
How to excel in all the roles you play		
• Specific advice for how to excel in the 21 roles that middle managers play (see chapter1).		
The mindset for leading effectively from the middle (Others-Oriented Leadership mindset)		
• Understand and apply the proven most effective mindset for leading from the middle. Learn how it builds on, but is still quite distinct from, the servant leadership mindset. See chapter 2 to ingrain, in specific ways: - **What you give** - **What you give up** - **What's a given** - **What you get**		
The skillset for leading effectively from the middle		
• Leverage the acronym AMPLIFY, discussed in detail in chapter 3: **Adaptability** (practice the six skill builds) **Meshing** (practice the three skill builds) **Political savviness** (take the Political Savviness Poll) **Locking in** (understand the four C's of Hyper-awareness: Constraints, Capacities, Capabilities, and Culture) **Influencing** (practice the six skill builds) **Fostering compromise** (recall the Golden Rules of Compromise) **You setting the tone** (remember the three rules of tone-setting)		
Leading up – your boss		
• Employ each step in The Managing Up Staircase revealed in chapter 4: - Step 1: Nature Before Nurture (know the five common mistakes in boss-subordinate relationship building) - Step 2: Understand the Asks (get crystal clear on expectations with nine key questions) - Step 3: Style Awareness (acknowledge the six key aspects of style)		

Figure 9.2 The Personal MAP (Middle Action Plan)

- Step 4: Get Personal (here's what to understand about your boss) - Step 5: Your House in Order (answer five questions to discern if you're on top of your business enough) - Step 6: Purposeful Support (know the six areas of purposeful support) - Specialty Steps (disagreeing with your boss, dealing with bad bosses, giving your boss feedback, managing multiple bosses)
Leading down – those who report to you
• Absorb chapter 5 to learn: - How to have great coaching conversations (using the Coaching Conversation Funnel and the Prescribe vs. Guide Spectrum) - How to pinpoint your employee's opportunity areas (with the six key points of pinpointing) - How to give transformative feedback (using eight fundamental plays, including the SHARES Feedback Framework) - How to teach in teachable moments (and spot the nine most common ones)
Leading across - teams
• Chapter 6 teaches you how to exponentially multiply your influence from the middle by leading a team with excellence. Discover: -The 15 telltale signs of the most successful teams (learn how to get them to materialize for your team) -How to galvanize your team around purpose (using the Purpose Pyramid-DRIVE tool) -How to shape the way employees experience your leadership team (utilizing the Leadership Team Equity Pyramid) -How to set powerful team goals (using the three Zones Test) -How to influence team behavior in times of poor results (understand the Waterfall Effect) -How to lead a remote team (leveraging the eight laws of effectively leading from a distance)
Influencing across - peers
• Grow your influence over peers (co-workers important to achieving your goals but that aren't necessarily on a formal team that you lead). Chapter 7 guides you via: The Pillars of Peer Influence: - Foundation 1: Cultivate a connection (just one sentence shows how) - Foundation 2: The Golden Rule of Influence (a baseline rule of thumb) - Pillar 1: Build the right reputation (become known for this set of things in particular) - Pillar 2: Make unexpected investments (learn/apply the two most powerful kinds) - Pillar 3: Hardwire their help (create direct influence over peers in these four ways) - Pillar 4: Get the approach right (six keys for your approach to influencing peers)

Figure 9.2 (*Continued*)

Leading change		
• Discover how to lead change effectively from your critical position in the middle. Chapter 8 shares: - The eight truths of leading change (they inform the change model that follows) - The EMC^2 Change Model * Phase 0: Change Readiness Assessment (follow four specific steps) * Phase 1: $\underline{E}$stablish change as a conduit (follow three specific steps and learn how to overcome five key barriers along the way) * Phase 2: $\underline{M}$ove employees from spectators to speculators (follow four specific steps and learn how to overcome four key barriers) * Phase 3: $\underline{C}$reate new habits 2. the squared denotes the doubling of effort needed at this stage (follow 3 specific steps and learn how to overcome 2 key barriers) - The One-on-One Change Conversation Guide (use the 12 prompts to enable a good change discussion, while being mindful of the Degrees of Empathy Scale)		

Figure 9.2 (*Continued*)

and overcoming all the unique challenges leaders in the middle face, knowing how to rock all the roles involved in leading from the middle, having the right mindset and skillset, and applying the right set of specific, specialty plays. You now have all of that at your fingertips.

So get leading from the middle to the best of your abilities: up, down, and across. Do so and you'll find all-around success.

ACKNOWLEDGMENTS

If you lead from the middle and you're reading this, you don't have time for a long page of acknowledgments. So I'll be brief, as long as you don't confuse my brevity for a lack of depth in appreciation.

Thank you to all the executives, up, down, across (and right in the middle) of so many organizations who contributed to this book by graciously granting interviews, filling out surveys, sitting in focus groups, or allowing me to observe "on the frontlines." Thank you to all the companies that give me the privilege of keynoting to their executives to share and shape all that I've learned. Thank you to my research partners who help me design studies that unearth real insight. Thank you to the faculty at Indiana University's School of Business for Executive Education, who grace me with staff membership and allow me to leverage my classes with executives as a living learning lab. Thanks to Procter & Gamble, my employer for so many years, which gave me the opportunity to rise in my own way, learning the entire time, from so many, on how it's done in all directions. Thanks to the team at *Inc.com*, who helped me hone my writing style to one more fit for the busy leader in the middle. Thanks so much to Mike Campbell at Wiley for seeing the potential in this book's idea, and helping me to shape and mold it into the playbook it has become. And as always, a hearty thank-you to my family members, those I live with and those distant, all of whom I can't live, create, and be inspired without.

ABOUT THE AUTHOR

Scott Mautz is a popular keynote speaker (scottmautz.com) and a former Procter & Gamble senior executive who successfully ran several of the company's largest multibillion-dollar businesses, all while transforming organizational health scores along the way. Scott is faculty at Indiana University's Kelley School of Business for Executive Education, where he teaches others-oriented leadership and the secret to sustaining employee engagement and high-performing organizations.

He was named a "CEO Thought-leader" by *The Chief Executives Guild* and a "Top 50 Leadership Innovator" by *Inc.com*, where he wrote a popular leadership/self-leadership column read by well over 1 million monthly readers. He's the author of *Make It Matter: How Managers Can Motivate by Creating Meaning* (March 2015), a book that has received many accolades including the 2106 Leadership Book of the Year—First Runner Up. His second book, *Find the Fire: Reignite Your Inspiration and Make Work Exciting Again* (October 2017), has likewise received multiple awards and much acclaim. He's also a LinkedIn Learning course instructor and CEO/founder of Profound Performance, a keynote, leadership training, and coaching company. Scott frequently appears in a variety of national media.

INDEX